HOW ARE
YOU DOING?

HOW ARE YOU DOING?

Stewart Dinnen

STL Books
PO Box 48, Bromley, Kent, England
PO Box 28, Waynesboro, Georgia, USA
PO Box 656, Bombay 1, India

* * * * * *

A  PUBLICATION

Copyright © 1984 Stewart Dinnen

First printing 1984, reprinted 1985

STL Books are published by Send The Light (Operation Mobilisation), PO Box 48, Bromley, Kent, England.

ISBN 0 903843 80 3

This edition published jointly with WEC Publications (Worldwide Evangelization for Christ), Bulstrode, Gerrards Cross, Bucks. SL9 8SZ, England.

Quotations from the Bible are from the New International Version, © 1978 by the New York International Bible Society, published in Great Britain by Hodder & Stoughton Ltd.

Cover illustration: Mary Evans Picture Library
Cover printed by Penderel Press Ltd, Croydon, Surrey

Made and printed in Great Britain by Hunt Barnard Printing Ltd, Aylesbury, Bucks.

Contents

About the Author

After obtaining an MA degree from Glasgow University, Stewart was in the Army for four years and was stationed in India, Burma and finally Malaya, where he served as Captain and Adjutant for the Malaya Command Signals.

Stewart and his wife Marie have served with WEC International for 35 years. They were firstly in Glasgow, then in the USA headquarters, and later leaders of the WEC training school in Tasmania, Australia for eighteen years.

Stewart is currently the International Secretary for the mission, which has over 1000 members working in 40 countries. He and Marie have two married daughters, and five grandchildren, all of them living in Australia.

All biblical quotations, unless otherwise noted, are taken from the *New International Version*.

Introduction

It's a great life! Working among young people on three continents may not be everybody's cup of tea, but it has been the task that God has given my wife Marie and me. We have been responsible for over thirty years for preparing volunteers for cross-cultural Christian service around the world. Most of them have come to us after completing some form of secular training, and our aim has then been to give them a thorough grounding in biblical principles and communication skills. We have specifically attempted to fill their hearts and minds with vital spiritual truths which they could grasp, experience, utilise and communicate to others.

You do not really know a truth until you are able to make it work in your own life, and you certainly cannot help anyone else to grasp it if you have not proved the reality of it for yourself. So as we learned more ourselves, then we were able to teach others. Through living, eating, serving and relaxing together (for we deliberately adopted a community lifestyle so that principles 'rubbed off') we saw many, many young people released, blessed and equipped for service. Today hundreds of them are serving Christ around the world and helping others to learn what we have taught them. Spiritual reproduction is the name of the game!

The chapters in this book first appeared in lecture notes and were then produced as leaflets. There has been a fairly widespread demand for them, particularly in Australia and New Zealand, so it was suggested that they could be put together as a book. The checklists may appear simple, but they are solid – boiled down, basic and biblical, if you like.

For that reason we ask you not to attempt to skim through too quickly – you need time to chew before you swallow, otherwise you will end up with spiritual indigestion.

If you have never seriously considered the four aspects of the cross in the New Testament, you will need time to think through and come to terms with the implications of them (page 47). If you have never systematically tried to discover God's will for your life, don't expect to master the twenty-seven steps in one day (page 34). If your faith is a bit unstable, you will need a few weeks to work through the twenty-two hints on how to develop it (page 66). In fact you could well give a year to the study of this book, taking a chapter every two weeks. It may be a good idea to keep a record of the lessons learnt and how you have actually applied them to your own life.

These checklists have been written in such a way as to appeal to your mind, your spirit and your will. The mind has to be enlightened – made aware of the existence of these principles; the spirit or heart needs to perceive or grasp the spiritual significance of them; and the will has to apply them. Total truth is totally demanding!

We hope you will discover, as hundreds of others have, that as Jesus says, 'You will know the truth, and the truth will set you free' (John 8:32). Trust the Holy Spirit, the Spirit of truth, to make it so for you.

Stewart Dinnen

21 *Marks of a Disciple*

Basic qualities

1. Right priorities

Consciously or unconsciously we each have a set of values that determines the practical decisions we make in our daily lives. The disciple has a clear commission from his Lord to 'seek first his kingdom and his righteousness' (Matt. 6:33). Two issues in this verse are of fundamental importance for every disciple – the kingdom of God (which is the company of all who have submitted to the lordship of Christ in every aspect of their being: body, soul and spirit) and God's righteousness (a quality of life which reflects the character of God). Submission and holy living – do you treat these as top priority in your life?

2. Simple lifestyle

Jesus' teaching in Matthew 6:25-33 clearly demands a simple lifestyle. This is strengthened by other warnings he gave about the danger of riches, and by Paul's words, 'People who want to get rich fall into temptation . . .' (1 Tim. 6:9). Have you honestly and sincerely accepted these words, 'But if we have food and clothing, we will be content with that' (1 Tim. 6:8)? Again, as in the first point, if our value system is right, we will be delivered from making material security and wealth ends in themselves. This was the factor that kept the rich young ruler out of the kingdom — 'He went away sad, because he had great wealth' (Mark 10:17-22).

3. Self-discipline

Paul tells Timothy, 'God did not give us a spirit of timidity, but a spirit of power, of love and of self-discipline', (literally a 'saved mind'), (2 Tim. 1:7). The instruction to each disciple is to 'carry his cross' (Luke 14:27), which simply means to accept a verdict of death to a self-centred lifestyle, so that every aspect of our life comes under the control of the Spirit. This is the essential difference between the Spirit-controlled disciple of 1 Corinthians 2:15 and the immature Christian of 3:1, who is still strongly influenced by personal preferences in daily life.

4. Purpose

The disciple is a Christian with a sense of commission. Having yielded himself to the lordship of Christ he does not rest until he is confident of being in the line of the Lord's purpose for his life. The New Testament has a lot to say about this:

• The will of God is satisfying. 'My food, said Jesus, is to do the will of him who sent me' (John 4:34).

• The will of God is suitable. Paul describes it as 'good, pleasing and perfect' (Rom. 12:2).

• The will of God is discernible. Paul says to the Colossian Christians that he is 'asking God to fill you with the knowledge of his will' (Col. 1:9).

• The will of God is pre-set. The Ephesian letter talks about the 'good works, which God prepared in advance for us to do' (Eph. 2:10).

• The will of God is achievable. The Hebrew letter says that God will 'equip you with everything good for doing his will' (Heb. 13:21).

• The will of God is eternal in its consequences. 'The

man who does the will of God lives for ever' (1 John 2:17).

It was said of Christ that he 'resolutely set out for Jerusalem' (Luke 9:51). Do you know where you are going or are you a drifter? What should your objectives be for the rest of this year? Next year?

5. Devotion

Devotion to Christ is impossible without a devotional life. To walk closely with Jesus necessitates spending time with him. The Psalmist speaks of praying in the morning, during the day and in the evening (Ps. 55:17); 1 Thessalonians 5:17 encourages us to 'pray continually' and in 2 Timothy Paul stresses that he should be 'a workman who does not need to be ashamed and who correctly handles the word of truth' (2:15). In fact a disciple is defined by Jesus as someone who obeys his teaching (John 8:31). These are the keys to strong spiritual growth.

6. Fruitfulness

Jesus also defines a disciple as one who bears fruit (John 15:8). 'Fruit' is the wholesome impact of our lives on others so that they want to be disciples too. A true disciple is an agent of change in other people's lives. Previously in verses 4 and 5 Jesus had said that fruitfulness is dependent on maintaining a vital relationship with himself. Sin, unbelief or self-sufficiency are some of the things that can hinder this. Read the whole of John 15 and you will find the secret not only of fruitfulness, but also of effective prayer, fellowship and patience under persecution.

The area of management

7. Sense of responsibility

The wise management of resources ('stewardship') is an essential quality in the disciple. The stories of Jesus in Matthew 25 highlight the concept of responsibility.

8. Use of time

Ephesians 5:16 teaches that we are to 'make the most of

the time' (RV). Treat time as a precious commodity. You have 960 minutes in every waking day. Once they are gone they cannot be retrieved!

9. Use of material resources

All that we have is given on trust. Nothing rightfully belongs to us. Even our wages are obtained on the basis of health and strength given by God. The point of the parable about talents in Matthew 25 is to teach the need for responsible and faithful handling of what is entrusted to us.

10. Giving

Part of the service-life of a disciple is wise giving. Jesus promised in Luke 6:38 that a giver will never be a loser. If the Israelites had to give a tenth under the demand of the Old Testament law, should we who know Christ give less? We are taught that 'a generous man will prosper' (Prov. 11:25) and that 'another withholds unduly but comes to poverty' (Prov. 11:24). Ask God to guide you in your giving. Your church fellowship should have priority, but think also of Christian missions that major in evangelism, church planting and the strengthening of believers.

11. Saving

It is an important part of stewardship to save, so that the disciple has resources for special crises or for needs in connection with Christian service or training. If you are seriously concerned about these eventualities, why not set aside a second tenth for such purposes?

12. Handling of the gospel

We are entrusted with the gospel and its spread throughout the world. Paul says he is entrusted with this commission (Acts 26:16), and Jesus clearly taught that we are to 'make disciples of all nations' (Matt. 28:19). What are you doing with the gospel? In local evangelism? In wider outreach? In evangelism to other peoples and nations?

13. Use of spiritual gifts

Every Christian is given at least one gift and we are told to serve one another by using it (1 Peter 4:10). Not to exercise the gift God has given is to rob your local fellowship of that which you – and only you – can contribute! (See page 81 for a further development of this theme.)

14. *Use of the body*
Even our physical body is given to us as a gift from God. Scripture teaches quite clearly that it is not our own (1 Cor. 6:19, 20) and Paul stresses the need to discipline the body (1 Cor. 9:27). Do you manage your body wisely, adopting patterns of living, sleeping, eating, working and recreating that are in line with good stewardship? Remember, if you are nine pounds overweight, this is equivalent to carrying a standard building brick around with you wherever you go!

Relationships

15. *Submission to authority*
Before we can truly experience the glorious liberty of belonging to God (Galatians 5:1), we have first to learn to submit to the authorities which God has placed in our lives. The Bible teaches us that discipleship will involve submission to these. (See page 42 for further teaching on this matter.)

16. *The local fellowship*
Of the twenty-two letters of the New Testament only five short ones were written to individuals. The rest were written to groups of Christians. The teaching of many passages such as Romans 12 – the 'submission' chapter, or 1 Corinthians 13 – the 'love' chapter, makes sense only when the disciple is reckoned to be part of a Christian group. Have you wholly identified with, and are you participating fully in the life of a local fellowship? This is God's method of maturing us in worship, fellowship and discipleship. Jesus said that the world will recognise us as disciples by the quality of our love for one another (John 13:35). This clearly implies that Jesus envisaged the establishment of local groups of believers recognised in the

community for the quality of their inter-relationships.

17.   The opposite sex

No other area of life has such potential for enrichment or wreckage. A sexual relationship between marriage partners is perfectly normal but sexual relationships outside of marriage or with another of the same sex is condemned as sinful (Romans 1:26-32). It is good to be a member of a mixed fellowship so that healthy relationships can be developed with both sexes. Make the issue of a life-partner a matter of consistent prayer.

18.   Missions

God has a place for mission groups as well as local church groups. In fact, personnel for the former should stem from the latter. Ask God to show you what society, country or ministry you are meant to support and pray for. Much blessing comes from giving missions a high priority in your life. Have you honestly faced up to the possibility that God may want you in some location other than where you are now?

19.   Your community

The gift of evangelism is not given to every disciple, but all are expected to be witnesses. Witnessing in the strength of the Spirit and in the leading of the Lord brings great release and joy. But Scripture warns us that the 'Fear of man will prove to be a snare' (Prov. 29:25). A close, obedient walk with Jesus is the key. John Hyde of India trusted the Lord to use him to win a person a day for a year, and he did. In fact, the second year he led two souls a day to Christ; and the next year four. Then he went to be with the Lord. A lovely way to go.

Two final words

20.   Career

This word does not appear in Scripture. Christ offered men a cross, not a career. Disciples should seek to equip themselves well by thorough vocational training, but it is impossible for a true disciple to set his sights on a career as an end in itself. In God's economy our life's work is related to the spiritual need of men and women, and even if God leaves us in a regular kind of job (in which there is always obligation to discharge our responsibilities in a God-glorifying way), the final reckoning will be in terms of the quality of our lives and our influence for Christ in other lives.

21. Conflict

Disciples are expected to know what spiritual conflict is all about. Paul urges Timothy to 'Endure hardship with us as a good soldier of Christ Jesus' (2 Tim. 2:3), and to 'fight the good fight' (1 Tim. 6:12). This is impossible unless the soldier knows how to use the weaponry described in Ephesians 6:10-18. There's a war on. Don't miss it.

Further reading

True Discipleship, William MacDonald, STL Books
The Cost of Commitment, John White, Inter-Varsity Press
Discipleship, David Watson, Hodder & Stoughton
No Turning Back, George Verwer, STL Books
Celebration of Discipline, Richard Foster, Hodder & Stoughton

In case of difficulty, books recommended for further reading can be obtained from STL Mail Order, PO Box 48, Bromley, Kent, England.

7 *Suggestions for a Vital Daily Time with God*

Your time with God is the most important part of your day. Satan knows this too, and he is out to keep you from having it; or else, while you are having it, to distract or discourage you. Here are some guidelines that will enable you to make the most of it.

1. Set a particular time aside

The best time is first thing in the morning. So go to bed the night before in time for adequate sleep; then you will be refreshed and ready the next morning. It is good to have a specific length of time laid aside, say thirty to forty minutes or an hour. Determine to use every minute of it effectively. Pray the night before about your time with God next morning. You will find it will go better. And what if you miss that time? The day is not lost. If you've been lazy, ask the Lord to forgive you and trust him implicitly as the day proceeds. If things have been beyond your control, he knows and you can rest in his faithfulness.

2. Start with praise

The Bible has lots to say about praise. In fact, many terms are used to describe different aspects of it, such as, worship, adoration and thanksgiving. Allow your mind to recapture something of the wonder of God's character, such as his mercy, love or faithfulness, and thankfully acknowledge all that he has done for you. Psalms 34, 37, 51 and 103 will help you. 'In everything, by prayer and petition, with thanksgiving, present your requests to God' (Phil. 4:6).

3. Seek a specific goal in Bible reading

As you turn to reading your Bible, try to avoid just reading for reading's sake. Have a goal. For instance, be looking for a promise to claim, or a principle to observe, or a warning to heed, or a command to obey. Don't pass over words you don't understand. You can get many helps to Bible study, such as daily readings, laymen's commentaries and Bible dictionaries. Plan to cover a certain amount a day, for example, one or two chapters. It is good to write down any spiritual truth that is a blessing to you. *Search the Scriptures* (IVP) gives thought-provoking questions and covers the whole Bible in three years.

'Blessed is the man [whose] delight is in the law of the Lord' (Ps. 1:1, 2).

'The law of the Lord is perfect,
reviving the soul.
The statutes of the Lord are trustworthy,
making wise the simple.
The precepts of the Lord are right,
giving joy to the heart.
The commands of the Lord are radiant,
giving light to the eyes.
The fear of the Lord is pure,
enduring for ever.
The ordinances of the Lord are sure,
and altogether righteous (Ps. 19:7-9).

'How can a young man keep his way pure? By living according to your word' (Ps. 119:9).

4. Make consistent use of a prayer list

Let your prayers be 'other-centred'. Many people with whom you have contact have spiritual needs. Pray consistently and be specific in your requests for relatives, workmates and fellowship group members. Ask God to lay on your heart the ones for whom you should pray regularly, and learn to pray in faith (Mark 11:22-24), expecting answers, and praising God for them.

5. Survey your circumstances

Pray about your day as it spreads before you – the problems you are going to meet, the pressures you are going to face, the people with whom you will be dealing. You will be very conscious of personal areas of weakness. Ask the Lord to show you how to cope by utilising your spiritual resources in Christ. Pray about your Christian witness and service, that you may be consistent, wise and loving.

6. Seek first the kingdom of God

Have a special place in your prayers for Christian workers both at home and overseas. Be a 'world Christian'. You can't pray for everybody, so take an interest in some specific part of God's work; get more information about it so that you can pray effectively.

7. Supplement Bible reading

Many fine books have been written to help Christians in their walk with the Lord. Always have a devotional book alongside your Bible and try to read a few chapters a week (not necessarily as part of your time with God, but at some point in the day). It is good to read biographies of famous Christians – their lives will bring a challenge and a blessing.

Things to do about this chapter

Evaluate your present daily time with God:
- consistently ineffective
- quality variable
- getting little from the word
- prayer deficiency

– feel consistently refreshed
– increasingly valuable
I could improve my daily time with God by:
  – fixing a definite time
  – listing prayer targets
  – planning systematic Bible study
  – widening prayer interest
I will read a book on prayer
I will purchase some Bible helps

Further reading

> *Prayer*, O Hallesby, Inter-Varsity Press
> *Prayer, Common Sense and the Bible*, Eric Fife, STL Books
> *People in Prayer*, John White, Inter-Varsity Press
> *The Practice of the Presence of God*, Brother Lawrence, Mowbrays
> *The Quiet Time*, Inter-Varsity Press (USA)

11 *Conditions for Answered Prayer*

1. Get rid of hindrances

A Christian worker was once asking the Lord to heal his wife of a sickness, but every time he prayed the face of another worker against whom he held a grudge appeared in his mind's eye. He finally wrote to this person apologising and putting his relationship right. Immediately his wife started to recover.

God cannot answer prayer if unconfessed sin remains in your heart, nor can he answer prayer if you are wilfully continuing in a sinful habit. Psalm 66:18 says, 'If I regard iniquity in my heart the Lord will not hear' (NASB). If we want to have access to God then we need to have 'clean hands and a pure heart' (Ps. 24:4).

2. Have a forgiving spirit

Many passages in the New Testament relate answered prayer to the spirit of forgiveness. Immediately after giving the 'model' prayer (called the Lord's prayer) in Matthew 6:9-13, Jesus stressed the issue of forgiveness. 'For if you forgive men when they sin against you, your heavenly Father will also forgive you. But if you do not forgive men their sins, your Father will not forgive your sins' (Matt.

6:14, 15). Jesus also says, 'And when you stand praying, if you hold anything against anyone, forgive him, so that your Father in heaven may forgive you your sins' (Mark 11:25).

3. *Pray in faith*

It is impossible to pray effectively without faith. 'Whatever you ask for in prayer, believe that you have received it, and it will be yours' (Mark 11:24). 'According to your faith will it be done to you' (Matt. 9:29). So often we say, 'But my faith is weak.' It is an encouragement to note that faith is capable of development. When Jesus was trying to get this idea over he used the picture of a mustard seed – an incredibly tiny pellet, yet capable of enormous growth (Matthew 17:20). However, faith is impossible unless we have the assurance that we are praying in God's will.

4. *The will of God*

For prayer to be effective, firstly we must have personally settled the issue of the will of God for our lives. We can't expect God to answer if we are living outside of his will. The issue of submission to the will of God is dealt with in Romans 12:1, 2, that teach if we submit ourselves to God and let him establish a new value system – a new way of looking at things – then we will discover the will of God and that it is good, pleasing and perfect.

In order to be sure that we are praying for that which is God's will, we need either a scriptural principle as a basis, or we need to wait on God until his Spirit gives us a peace in our heart about praying along a certain line. For example, if we know that two Christians have had a quarrel, we can pray on the authority of God's word that they be reconciled because it is God's purpose, as stated in Romans 12:10, that Christians should be devoted to one another in brotherly love.

5. *Agreement*

If we are praying with others, a key to answered prayer is

that those involved first ensure that they are really in agreement regarding their prayer objective. Jesus says, 'If two of you on earth agree about anything you ask for, it will be done for you . . .' (Matt. 18:19). Take time then, to talk things over, so that this basic principle is established.

6. Living in union with Jesus

In John 15 Jesus makes it very clear that another prerequisite to answered prayer is to be living in a close relationship with him. 'If you remain in me and my words remain in you, ask whatever you wish, and it will be given you' (verse 7).

What does it mean to have his words remaining in you? It simply means that we put tremendous importance into knowing and following the teachings of Jesus, and this will mean a daily dip into the word so that its truths provide a subconscious layer of influence upon all you say and do.

There is no other issue of greater significance for any disciple than the quality of his relationship with the master. The closer you are, the smaller your problems. The further away you are, the bigger the hassles.

7. Don't be double-minded

The epistle of James pinpoints a weakness that must be dealt with if the disciple is going to be effective in prayer; it is called 'double-mindedness' – thinking in two directions. 'He who doubts is like a wave of the sea, blown and tossed by the wind. That man should not think he will receive anything from the Lord' (James 1:6,7). Have specific goals in prayer – clear objectives – and stick to them.

8. Pray with persistence

It is one thing to pray around a need; it is another to pray through to the point where you have strong faith and confidence that your prayer is going to be answered. Jesus tells the story of a man who badly needed some bread from his neighbour because some friends had come in the middle of the night. He draws the picture of his shameless persistence and of course he gets what he wants (Luke

11:5-9). Then Jesus applies this to the listeners and urges them to ask, seek, knock.

Why do we have to pray like this? Is God reluctant to hear and answer? Of course not. Two factors come into play. Firstly, Satan stands against us, and often our praying clears away the opposition. Sometimes there is another factor – the unbelief of our own hearts. Sometimes prayer is the only expedient that will free us from our own unbelief. A man once said to Jesus, 'I do believe; help me overcome my unbelief' (Mark 9:24) – a curious mixture, but very true to life.

9. *Pray with authority*

We often picture ourselves in the role of beggars when we pray. But Jesus doesn't mean us to feel like that. He says, 'ask in my name' (John. 15:16). This doesn't mean just 'tacking on' the name of Jesus at the end of our prayer. 'Name' in Scripture means, 'authority, prestige, character'. Jesus was saying, 'Pray with my delegated authority'. In other words, 'See yourselves as my representatives and act accordingly.'

In Mark 11:24 Jesus teaches that we should actually address any obstacle in the way of our prayer-objective, and demand that it move off. This is praying with authority.

10. *Unity of spirit*

'How good and pleasant it is when brothers live together in unity . . . there the Lord bestows his blessing' (Ps. 133:1, 3). If the Holy Spirit is being grieved through lack of unity, answered prayer becomes an impossibility. Undercurrents of murmuring, dissatisfaction, criticism and backbiting grieve and hinder the Holy Spirit. 'Be patient, bearing with one another in love. Make every effort to keep the unity of the Spirit' (Eph. 4:2, 3).

To husbands, Peter says, 'Be considerate as you live with your wives, and treat them with respect . . . so that nothing will hinder your prayers' (1 Pet. 3:7).

11.   Pray to the Father by the Spirit in the name of the Son
We have already dealt with praying in Jesus' name. Our prayers should be addressed to the Father: 'Do it all in the name of the Lord Jesus, giving thanks to God the Father through him' (Col. 3:17); 'Present your requests to God' (Phil. 4:6). And our prayers should be with reliance on the Holy Spirit: 'Pray in the Spirit on all occasions' (Eph. 6:18); 'The Spirit helps us in our weakness' (Rom. 8:26).

A staggering thought – the Trinity is involved when we pray.

Further reading

George Muller: Delighted in God, Roger Steer, STL Books
Anything You Ask, Colin Urquhart, Hodder & Stoughton
Power Through Prayer, E M Bounds, Zondervan
What Happens When Women Pray, Evelyn Christensen, Victor Books
Rees Howells, Intercessor, Norman Grubb, Lutterworth Press

7 *Methods of Bible Study*

1. The vacuum cleaner
The cleaner's nozzle advances steadily across the carpet picking up all in its path. So you too may work steadily through a particular book of the Bible, accumulating spiritual truth and marking your Bible as you go. However, this method lacks 'focus' and is not the best for consistent and effective study.

2. The bread slicer
Read a whole book with a view to slicing it into chunks (several chapters) and giving each chunk a title which reflects the subject material. To give you an example here is an outline of the book of Romans based on this method.
ROMANS
General Title: God's Way of Righteousness
Chunk 1 Chapters 1-5 True righteousness revealed
Chunk 2 Chapters 6-8 True righteousness realised
Chunk 3 Chapters 9-11 True righteousness for the Jews
Chunk 4 Chapters 12-16 True righteousness reproduced
in practical life

3. The blood hound
Just as a blood hound follows a trail by picking up the

scent you can 'follow a trail' through a book by picking up every mention of a particular idea or theme. For instance a fruitful study in I John is to pick out all the verses that deal with fellowship and caring for one another. Here are some of them: 1:3, 6, 7; 2:9-11; 3:14-17, 23; 4:11, 20, 21; 5:16.

4. The octopus

The tentacles of an octopus reach out in all directions, under a central control. With the help of a concordance you can reach out through the Scriptures gathering material which relates to a particular topic. Choose a fairly limited topic to start with, otherwise you will be swamped. For example, instead of studying 'the love of God' try 'forgiveness'; instead of studying 'money' study 'giving'.

5. The pigeon hole

The 'pigeon hole' is a device for separating mail for different people. Approach the Scriptures with predetermined 'pigeon holes' in your mind for isolating specific truths. For instance, you may study a book or part of a book to discover all the promises it contains, all the commands, all the spiritual principles, all the warnings, or all that reveals more of Christ or the Holy Spirit. Accumulate findings in a tabulated notebook.

Here is a study on the commands in Ephesians 4:

Verse 1	Live a life worthy of the calling you have received.
Verse 2	Be completely humble and gentle.
Verse 2	Be patient, bearing with one another in love.
Verse 3	Make every effort to keep the unity of the Spirit through the bond of peace.
Verse 17	You must no longer live as the Gentiles do, in the futility of their thinking.
Verse 25	Each of you must put off falsehood and speak truthfully to his neighbour.
Verse 26	In your anger do not sin.
Verse 26	Do not let the sun go down while you are still angry.
Verse 27	Do not give the devil a foothold.

Verse 28 He who has been stealing must steal no longer, but must work.

Verse 29 Do not let any unwholesome talk come out of your mouths, but only what is helpful for building others up.

Verse 30 Do not grieve the Holy Spirit of God.

Verse 31 Get rid of all bitterness, rage and anger, brawling and slander, along with every form of malice.

Verse 32 Be kind and compassionate to one another, forgiving each other, just as in Christ God forgave you.

6. *The zoom lens*

A zoom lens brings a distant object into close focus. Study all references to a particular Bible character so that you can examine the life in detail. Do not start with a well-known person like David, Peter or Paul but start with someone like Barnabas. There are just twelve verses or short passages covering his life and they make a most rewarding study. Here are the references: Acts 4:36; 9:27; 11:22, 25, 30; 12:25; 13:1-7; 1 Cor. 9:6; Gal. 2:1, 9, 13; Col. 4:10.

7. *The oil rig*

The oil rig is a superstructure that enables the drillers to go deep into the earth layer below layer. For the Christian many resources are available to help him get down into the meaning of Bible verses and words. Using aids such as an interlinear Greek/English version, Vine's Dictionary of New Testament Words, or a Bible Dictionary, study a verse in depth. Find the basic meaning of each word. Note verb tenses. Here is a sample study on Romans 5:1, 'Therefore, since we have been justified through faith, we have peace with God through our Lord Jesus Christ.'

Therefore – a link with the end of the previous chapter (Note: no chapter divisions exist in the Greek New Testament). Jesus' death, according to 4:25, was an offering to God for our sins, i.e. our guilt was dealt with.

His resurrection was a proof that God accepted his sacrifice; therefore we who trust in that sacrifice have confidence that we are acceptable to God.

justified – from a Greek word *dikaioo* which means 'to declare righteous' (Vine's Dictionary, page 285). It does not mean 'make righteous', but to accept as righteous – given a status of rightness before God.

through Faith – justification is obtained through trust in the completed work of Christ on the cross. The ground of our justification is Christ's death and resurrection. The means of obtaining it is our faith. Vine says faith has three elements: a) conviction about, b) commitment to, c) conduct in line with a) and b) (Vine, page 71).

peace with God – 'Harmonised relationships between God and man' (Vine, page 170). This peace with God is the result of the exercise of faith in Christ's saving work on the cross. 'He came and preached peace to you who were far away' (Eph. 2:17).

Lord Jesus Christ – Lord – *kurios* – 'Master'

Jesus – *iesous* – 'Saviour'

Christ – *christos* – 'Anointed one'

Further reading

Understanding the Bible, John Stott, Scripture Union
Let the Bible Speak, John Balchin, Inter-Varsity Press
I Believe in Revelation, Leon Morris, Eerdmans
Every Man a Bible Student, J E Church, Paternoster Press
How To Study the Bible for Yourself, Tim La Haye, Harvest House

20 Reasons for Believing the Bible Is the Word of God

1. From earliest times to the development of the Church at the end of the first century AD, God consistently caused his revealed word to be written down, so it is logical to believe that he intended that these Scriptures were to be a revelation of his nature and a guide to human conduct.

2. Although the Bible has many writers from all walks of life, all have a common purpose in portraying a holy, righteous, all-powerful God who acts out of love towards man.

3. Although the subject matter of the sixty-six books of the Bible is infinitely varied, there is a unity in its revelation of God and his redemptive purpose in Christ.

4. A unique harmony exists between the two parts of the Bible. Someone has said, 'The New is in the Old concealed: the Old is in the New revealed.'

5. Christ believed the Old Testament Scriptures implicitly and entirely; he submitted himself to their teachings, fulfilled them, and warned against detracting from them.

6. The Apostles accepted the authority of the Old Testament and recognised Christ as its fulfilment. Peter in

Acts 2:16 says, 'This is what was spoken by the prophet Joel . . .'

7.   From the third century AD the Christian Church has universally recognised the unique quality of the inspired Scriptures (known as the 'Canon').

8.   Paul writing under the inspiration of the Holy Spirit said, 'All Scripture is God-breathed' (2 Tim. 3:16). As it is a witness to truth in other matters it is consistent to accept what it says about itself.

9.   Although the idea of a 'supreme being' exists around the world, the history of heathenism fails to disclose the concept of a pure, holy God kindly disposed to the human race. The Bible is the unique written revelation about the character of God.

10.   The Holy Spirit who witnesses in the Christian to the reality of Christ, also witnesses to the truth of God's word.

11.   Not to accept the Bible for what it claims to be presents the problem of finding some alternative authority on which to base moral judgments. The alternatives – human reason or tradition – are inadequate because human nature is fallible.

12.   No other book combines such beauty, wisdom and lofty morality as the Bible. No book gives such a clear description of the human heart. Yet its basic message is simple and easy to understand.

13.   In every culture men's lives, no matter how degraded, have been transformed by the power of its message – a proof that it is God's supernatural word written to meet the needs of the human heart. In simple words, it works.

14.   The existence of the Church, the story of foreign missions and the innumerable experiences of answered prayer are indisputable evidence of the truth of its message.

15.   When the Church has failed to translate, study, and distribute the Scriptures, it has withered. The church of North Africa in the early centuries had great

Christians – but they failed to translate the Scriptures, with the result that it did not have the strength to resist the invasion of Islam.

16. Every true spiritual revival has been accompanied by a return to the centrality of the Scriptures.

17. Bible believers have no basic problem about 'unity' in faith and action – witness their involvement (irrespective of denomination) in such activities as community evangelistic crusades and conventions, evangelical foreign missions, and relief agencies like TEAR Fund and World Vision.

18. Prophecies of Scripture have been and are being fulfilled (such as the destruction of Jerusalem, and the return of Jews to Palestine).

19. Archaeological discoveries have consistently confirmed the truth of the Bible.

20. The Bible has survived over the centuries in spite of every form of opposition, suppression and destruction.

Further reading

God Has Spoken, Jim Packer, Hodder & Stoughton

The Battle for the Bible, Harold Lindsell, Zondervan

The New Testament Documents, F F Bruce, Inter-Varsity Press

Authority, D M Lloyd-Jones, Banner of Truth

The Authority of the Bible, Jack Cottrell, Baker Book House

Evidence That Demands a Verdict, Josh McDowell, Campus Crusade

27 *Steps Towards the Will of God*

1.   Withdraw from all known sin. We can't expect to have our prayers answered if we have not dealt with unconfessed sin. Isaiah tells us that sin separates us from God (Isaiah 59:1, 2). So confess it, and seek God's will as a cleansed person. John says in his First Epistle that God 'is faithful and just and will forgive us our sins and purify us' if we come in genuine confession (1 John 1:9).

2.   Willingness to submit to the Lord's direction. We must first settle the issue of commitment to discipleship and be willing to accept the principle of the cross as Christ explains in Luke 14:27; 'Anyone who does not carry his cross and follow me cannot be my disciple.'

3.   Want to know. What is your heart's desire? Is the will of God your highest priority? Jesus says, 'Seek first his kingdom' in Matthew 6:33 and promises that if we do this all the things that we normally consider as priorities – the 'basics' of living – will be given to us.

4.   Wait on God. This involves keeping the matter consistently before God in prayer, and thinking things through in his presence. Acts 13 describes how a group of

men decided to fast and wait in God's presence. As they did so the Holy Spirit showed them what to do (verses 1-3).

5.   Wholehearted trust. Proverbs 3:5, 6, says, 'Trust in the Lord with all your heart . . . in all your ways acknowledge him and he will make your paths straight.' Do not be 'a double-minded man, unstable in all he does' (James 1:8). Trust God implicitly and totally.

6.   Wear Christ's yoke. Christ invites us to share a yoke with him (Matthew 11:29). What is the significance? A yoke is a device for keeping two animals together as they pull a plough. In practice, a less experienced animal learns from its partner (a) through close contact, (b) being guided in the right direction, (c) moving forward at the right pace. The spiritual application is obvious.

7.   Word of God. The Holy Spirit will never lead you contrary to the truths of God's word. The Psalmist says, 'I have hidden your word in my heart that I might not sin against you' (Ps. 119:11). Beware of isolating special verses and taking them as 'guidance'.

8.   Weighing the circumstances. Remember Satan's purpose is to hinder and deflect us from God's will, as Paul infers in 1 Thessalonians 2:18 and 1 Timothy 4:1. And remember too that Satan has evil spirits who want to deceive us (1 Timothy 4:1). So learn how to interpret the happenings of life while being sensitive to the Holy Spirit.

9.   Wisdom of counsellors. Share your concern with spiritually-minded seniors whose opinion you value. Very often confirmation comes through their reaction or advice. 'A wise man listens to advice' (Prov. 12:15).

10.   Ways of guidance for others. Study the manner in which God has guided his servants. You will find many instances in Scripture, church history and biography. Take note of the experiences of modern disciples like Brother Andrew, Dr Helen Roseveare and Bruce Olson.

11.   Wetting the fleece. When it is hard to distinguish

between personal feelings and the Spirit's confirmation, ask God to do something objective outside yourself, as an indication of his will. Gideon was very unsure, so he asked God to cause a fleece which he placed on the threshing floor overnight to be covered with dew next morning, and the surrounding area to be dry. It happened. Next night he reversed the request and that happened (Judges 6:37-39).

12.   Write out a balance sheet. It is good to sit down with a sheet of paper divided into two columns and list the reasons for and against taking a particular decision.

13.   Win a prayer partner (or group). If the issue is of long term significance, it is an excellent idea to share your need with someone who will stand with you in positive faith for God's mind to be revealed. 'For where two or three come together in my name, there am I with them' (Matt. 18:20).

14.   Work to established spiritual principles. Often specific guidance is not needed because the issue is covered by a biblical principle. For example, 'Obey your leaders and submit to their authority' (Heb. 13:17) and 'Seek first his kingdom' (Matt. 6:33).

15.   Watch for the Spirit's equipment. This is specially relevant to those concerned about Christian service. The Holy Spirit's gifts can be an indication of the avenue you should take. (See page 81 on spiritual gifts for an explanation.)

16.   Witness of the Holy Spirit. The Holy Spirit confirms by an inner assurance what God is showing you in other ways. Paul wrote, 'Let the peace of Christ rule [be the umpire] in your hearts' (Col. 3:15). At the same time beware of a peace which is simply the absence of tension following a time of decision-making.

17.   Wage war against selfish desires. Beware of decisions that are dominated by the desire for affluence,

ease or the fulfilment of personal ambitions. Paul warns the Romans, 'Do not conform any longer to the pattern of this world' (12:2).

18. Be wary of counterfeits. Satan has seducing (misleading) spirits. Often the good is the enemy of the best. For example, don't make the excuse that the choir can't manage without you if the Holy Spirit is convicting you about going to Bible college.

19. The world can allure. Ensure that your decision is not dominated by a desire for position, security or acclaim. 1 John 2:16 identifies the world with 'the cravings of sinful man, the lust of his eyes and the boasting of what he has and does.'

20. Watch the subtlety of the rational mind. Don't tackle a spiritual issue with humanistic resources. Proverbs 3:5 warns us about being dependent on our own understanding.

21. Wisdom that is sanctified and used with spiritual discernment can help determine the right course. For instance, Paul saw Timothy's potential as a future Christian worker and asked him to join his team (Acts 16:1-3). 'The wisdom that comes from heaven is first of all pure; then peaceloving, considerate, submissive, full of mercy and good fruit, impartial and sincere' (James 3:17).

22. Withstand fear. 'Perfect love drives out fear' (1 John 4:18). God is a loving heavenly Father. His will is the best thing that could happen to us. What to fear most is moving outside the security of his perfect will.

23. Weakness does not disqualify. Christians often resist God's will because they don't feel adequate for that to which God is calling them. But his commission carries the guarantee of his enabling. In Philippians 4:13 Paul says, 'I can do everything through him' and Hebrews 13:20, 21 says, 'May the God of peace . . . equip you with everything good for doing his will.'

24.   World need and Christ's command about meeting that need with the message of the gospel, as stated in Matthew 28:18-20, constitute guidance in principle for every Christian. Once the principle is accepted the issues of how to serve, where to serve, and with whom to serve can become matters for specific direction.

25.   Waiting in complete passivity is not biblical. Guidance won't just 'arrive'. Use the means given in a positive way. Psalm 32:9 says, 'Do not be like the horse or mule, which have no understanding but must be controlled by bit and bridle'.

26.   Working to a deadline can be a healthy exercise. If the answer is needed by a certain date, confidently assert your expectancy that the Lord will give an indication of his will by that time. Jesus sets the pattern in Mark 11:24, 'Whatever you ask for in prayer, believe that you have received it, and it will be yours.'

27.   Walk by faith. Be prepared to step out in faith. If you know God has given a sense of leading, then the only course is to launch out, trusting him implicitly. As Jesus said to Peter in Luke 5:4, 'Put out into deep water'.

Further reading

> *Day by Day Guidance*, Paul Little, Falcon
> *Give Up Your Small Ambitions*, Michael Griffiths, Inter-Varsity Press
> *Where Do We Go from Here, Lord?*, Zac Poonen, Tyndale
> *Guidance, Some Biblical Principles*, Oliver Barclay, Inter-Varsity Press
> *Knowing God's Will and Doing It*, J Grant Howard, Zondervan

21 Lessons on How To Avoid Becoming a Missionary

1.   Skilfully avoid the command in John 4:35 to take a long hard look at the fields. This is not only depressing but it is unsettling, and could lead to genuine missionary concern.

2.   Have a good healthy (socially legitimate) target ahead of you, such as higher qualifications, promotion, bigger home, better car, or higher salary.

3.   Get married as soon as possible so you can devote your life to the socially accepted norm of settling down, raising a family and providing for old age.

4.   Stick to generalities. Never allow the stark needs of specific mission fields make an impact on you. Use vague terms like 'the heathen', 'missions', or 'the unevangelised world'.

5.   Never expose yourself to personal contact with missionaries. Their testimonies are disturbing, and the situations they describe tend to contrast with the materialistic living of the western world.

6.   Insist that your theology of guidance rules out any possibility of specific personal direction from God.

7.   Keep busy. Always bow to the tyranny of the urgent and avoid concentration on the importance of the

strategic. You can even keep busy in Christian work (as long as it's done in your own strength).

8. If you've been wrongly criticised, had a dirty trick played on you, or have otherwise come out the loser, maintain your hurt; stay offended. People with a chip on their shoulder don't usually have time for the needs of others.

9. Rationalise about missions. After all, if 55,000 missionaries can't finish the job, what difference will you make?

10. Develop a closed-door mentality. Remember Albania, Mongolia, North Korea, iron and bamboo curtains and turned down visas. (Forget the 100 plus countries still open to missionaries.)

11. Develop a 'national-church-can-do-it' attitude. Never investigate the percentage of the population which they constitute, or the severe limitations of their resources.

12. Focus your attention exclusively on the evils of your own society. All fair-minded Christians will applaud your concern about violence, drugs and abortion. 'Mission begins at home' and make sure it finishes there too.

13. Always keep in mind your own past failures. It is unreasonable to expect you will ever be any better. This means never study the lives of Abraham, Moses, David, Jonah, Peter or Mark who were all drop-outs at one stage, but didn't stay that way.

14. Always look at missionaries as super-spiritual people with tremendous gifts and saintly characters. This will heighten your sense of inadequacy and remove any guilt complex about not being one of them.

15. Avoid all books that emphasise the ability of the Holy Spirit to change lives (including your own) and to provide power for service.

16. You can always claim you don't have 'the missionary gift' and since you have not been in a cross-cultural communicating ministry no one can prove you are wrong. (On the other hand you can't prove yourself right.)

Finally, if you do become a little concerned about missionary work:

17.   Insist that the slot you are to fill is exactly tailored to your qualifications. (That way, you'll never find an opening.)

18.   Go out right away without any training. You'll soon be home again, but no one will be able to blame you for not trying!

19.   Start worrying about money and the impossibility of surviving in a country with an annual one hundred per cent inflation rate. (The Lord is *not* greater than inflationary pressures.)

20.   Listen to those who feel you are indispensable where you are, and that your local church can't do without you.

21.   Never sing the hymn, 'Onward Christian Soldiers'. Always substitute the following version:

> 'Mark time Christian heroes;
> Never go to war.
> Stop and mind the babies
> Playing on the floor.
> Wash and dress and feed them
> Forty times a week,
> Till they're roly poly
> Puddings, so to speak.'   (C T Studd)

Further reading

True Discipleship, William MacDonald, STL Books
The Chocolate Soldier, C T Studd, WEC
Going Places, Elizabeth Goldsmith, STL Books
Move out, Michael Duncan, STL Books
Ten Sending Churches, M Griffiths (ed.), MARC

10 5 Authorities To Respect and Authorities To Exercise

Respecting authority

Who (or what) runs your life? The question of authority is a fundamental one for every Christian. This chapter seeks to clarify what Scripture teaches on this subject. Ten legitimate determining sources can be recognised in the word of God.

1. The sovereignty of God the Father

The disciple is called to recognise that God is in control of his every circumstance. To rebel, to mistrust, to grumble about what is happening to you, is to refuse to acknowledge God's sovereign purpose in your life. Romans 8:28 says that, 'In all things God works for the good of those who love him.' God is not the author of evil, but, so that we may prove him, he will allow us to feel pressure. The key is praise. The Psalmist says, 'I will extol the Lord at all times; his praise will always be on my lips' (34:1). When we praise God we are in effect saying, 'I recognise that God is in charge; I may not like this but he has a purpose in it, for which I praise him.'

2. The lordship of Christ

The path of discipleship commences with the life being positively committed in faith to the control of Christ. 'Offer your bodies as living sacrifices, holy and pleasing to God' (Rom. 12:1). This is the cross principle – the termination of an independent lifestyle by a daily walk in the risen life of Jesus. Paul summed it up well when he said in Galatians 2:20, 'I have been crucified with Christ and I no longer live, but Christ lives in me.'

3. The authority of the word

In practical terms the final source of direction in life has to be one of these: humanism – man's ability to reason and evaluate; tradition – either of society or of the Church; or the will of God as revealed in the Scriptures which he has inspired. 2 Timothy 3:16 says that these were given by God and are profitable for teaching, rebuke, correction and training in righteousness, so that the disciple can be thoroughly equipped for Christian service. We are not to ignore the value of reason or the guidance of those over us in the Lord, but the Scriptures stand supreme.

4. The control of the Spirit

'Those who are led by the Spirit of God are sons of God' (Rom. 8:14). Discipleship will involve sensitivity to the Spirit's control. It is interesting that the Greek word for 'obey' is *hupakouo*, which literally means 'to hear under', i.e. 'to be sensitive to the voice from above'. The Scriptures give broad principles for Christian living, and the Spirit checks and encourages in personal and practical issues. In Colossians 3:15 Paul says, 'Let the peace of Christ rule in your hearts'. This peace is created by the Holy Spirit when believers are in line with Christ's purpose. The word translated 'rule' (Greek – *brabeuo*) actually means 'to act as an umpire, arbitrate'.

5. The function of the government

Romans 13:1 tells us to be subject to governmental authority and the representatives of government. 'Everyone must submit himself to the governing authorities'. 1 Peter 2:13-15 confirms this and stresses the value of our testimony when we do so. 'By doing good you . . . silence the ignorant talk of foolish men.'

6. The place of parents

'Obey your parents . . . Honour your father and mother.'

Ephesians 6:1, 2 confirms the Old Testament teaching that
children are to submit to their parents. No age limit
appears to be given, but obviously this applies at least until
we come to years of personal accountability. Disciples
should be willing to submit to the will of unconverted
parents (except when doing so would deny a biblical
principle).

7. The position of leaders

Hebrews 13:7, 17 reveal that part of discipleship is to
recognise the position of leaders in the local church. These
men are (or should be) appointed for their spiritual
maturity and wisdom. They are God's provision to guide
less mature people in the things of the Lord, and the affairs
of the local church.

8. Laws of nature

God has placed man within the bounds of his universe and
has established physical laws with which he is meant to
comply. For example: (a) requirement of rest and sleep; to
restrict this for any reason reduces our abilities and
efficiency; (b) man is created a heterosexual being.
Homosexuality is a deviation. The horrific passage in
Romans 1:24-32 catalogues the errors of departing from
God's norms.

9. The rights of an employer

Scripture teaches the obligations of the employee to the
employer and the employer to the employee. A disciple's
witness at work revealed through his attitude to those in
authority is a significant factor. In a day of lowering
standards in business, many a disciple's integrity has led to
promotion and increased responsibility. Ephesians 6:5 says
that he is to serve his employer with the same attitude as he
would serve Christ.

10. The position of other believers

We are encouraged to submit to one another out of love
and respect. Romans 12:10 says, 'Be devoted to one
another . . . Honour one another above yourselves.' There

is a special emphasis on young people submitting to those over them in the Lord. 1 Peter 5:5 says, 'Young men . . . be submissive to those who are older. Clothe yourselves with humility towards one another'.

Exercising authority

Those who qualify for the exercise of authority are those who have first learned to submit. Here are some areas where the disciple is entrusted with authority.

1. Praying with authority
The disciples were taught by the Lord to pray with his delegated authority ('in my name' appears five times in John 14-16). The meaning is that if our relationship to him is right – the 'abiding' of John 15:7 (AV) – we will be expressing his will in our prayers. Prayer for the disciple was never meant to be simple expressions of a vague hope – it is intended to express a disciple's conviction regarding the Lord's intent. We co-operate with God by exercising this authority.

2. Resisting Satan
James 4:7 ('Submit . . . to God. Resist the devil, and he will flee . . .') and 1 Peter 5:9 ('Resist him, standing firm in the faith') teach us that, once we are totally submissive to the will of God, we have authority to resist Satan's attacks. It is necessary first to be able to recognise satanic pressure so that we can then assert our superior position over him as disciples of Christ. (See page 55 for a further explanation of this.)

3. Dealing with evil spirits
The ground of our authority over Satan is also the reason why we can demand the withdrawal of Satan's forces, or evil spirits, in the name of Jesus. This confrontation is referred to in Ephesians 6:12, 'For our struggle is not against flesh and blood, but against . . . the powers of this dark world and against the spiritual forces of evil'. Christ exposed and exorcised many demons (for example, in Luke

9:42 it says Jesus rebuked an evil spirit). He gave his disciples the same authority over Satan's agents.

4. Proclaiming the gospel

Disciples are not meant to evangelise from a position of mere persuaders or suppliants. They are to proclaim with the authority of those who have proved the reality of the message, through the change in their own lives. Matthew 28:18-20 teaches that the disciple involved in evangelism is to do so with the assurance that he is going forth in the Lord's strength and with his authority. 'All authority in heaven and on earth has been given to me. Therefore go and make disciples . . .' We have an authoritative message and testimony: 'Jesus saves; he has saved us, and he told us to tell you, which we now do, in his strength.'

5. Leading the Church

Mature disciples are given authority in the affairs of the local church. This is not to be carried out in a harsh and autocratic way – 'not lording it over those entrusted to you, but being examples to the flock' (1 Pet. 5:3). The qualifications for appointment to such responsibilities are given in 1 Timothy 3 and Titus 1. Elders are given specific authority to pray in faith for sick believers who request them to do so, 'anoint . . . with oil in the name of the Lord' (James 5:14, 15). (See page 126 for further teaching on leadership responsibility.)

Further reading

Knowing God, Jim Packer, Hodder & Stoughton

The Knowledge of the Holy, A W Tozer, STL Books

Freedom and Discipline, Jerram Barrs, Inter-Varsity Press

The Authority of the Believer, A J McMillan, Christian Publications

Touching the Invisible, Norman Grubb, Lutterworth Press

4 *Dimensions of the Cross*

Many Christians only understand one dimension of the cross and fail to perceive the New Testament teaching on the other three, with the result that their experience is shallow and their service very defective. This chapter seeks firstly to explain the four dimensions and then to show their practical significance.

1. Salvation

This is the one concept that every person needs to understand before the new birth can take place. 'For the message of the cross is foolishness to those who are perishing, but to us who are being saved it is the power of God' (1 Cor. 1:18). The 'message of the cross' is of course the fact that Christ, in his dying on the cross, was bearing our sins. 'He is the atoning sacrifice for our sins . . . also for the sins of the whole world' (1 John 2:2), and as a risen Christ he is ready to enter our hearts and change us when we come to him in repentance and faith. 'If anyone is in Christ, he is a new creation' (2 Cor. 5:17).

2. Liberation

'I have been crucified with Christ and I no longer live, but Christ lives in me' (Gal. 2:20). Paul here uses the idea of

crucifixion to convey the thought that his coming to Christ
meant that the old Paul 'dropped out', ceased to exist, as
far as domination by sin and selfishness is concerned, and
he has 'come up' in a new relationship – an 'in-Christ'
relationship which makes him a new person with new
capabilities. So the cross is the great divide between self-
oriented living, and Christ-related living. Peter says this
too in 1 Peter 2:24, 'He himself bore our sins in his body
on the tree, so that we might die to sins and live for
righteousness.'

But this truth only becomes effective, real and
experiential when we see, recognise and agree with this
verdict, namely that we become 'dead men' to independent
living and 'living men' in a Christ-controlled relationship.
We don't come there easily. The flesh will do anything but
die. It will give, work, travel a thousand miles in the name
of Christian service, but submit to the cross? No way! It is
only after we clearly see our self-directed self that we come
afresh to the cross and see it as a place of liberation.

As Hugh Evan Hopkins says in *The Law of Liberty in
the Spiritual Life* our part consists in getting down into the
death of Christ. His part is to live out his own life in us.
Let us see that we are not seeking to partake of the life
without going down into his death. He goes on to point out
that many think that 'having seen the cross in its atoning
and justifying aspect, we have now passed beyond it and
have left it behind,' but the truth is that we have a need to
bring ourselves to identify with Christ at the cross and to
know a new level of dealing and breaking that then allows
the sweetness of Jesus to flow through us in a new way.
Wine comes from crushed grapes. Paul says in Philippians
3:10, 'I want to know Christ and the power of his
resurrection and the fellowship of sharing in his sufferings,
becoming like him in his death'.

Paul says in Galatians 6:14, 'May I never boast except in
the cross . . . through which the world has been crucified
to me, and I to the world.' Paul sees the cross as the
separating mechanism. He, by accepting the cross

principle, has become a dead man as far as the world is concerned and the world has become a dead force as far as he is concerned.

Do you know the principle of the cross as well as the event of the cross?

3. *Discipline*
'We always carry around in our body the death of Jesus' (2 Cor. 4:10); 'We who are alive are always being given over to death for Jesus' sake' (2 Cor. 4:11) and 'I die every day – I mean that, brothers' (1 Cor. 15:31).

This is the repetitive cross – the pattern of the cross, as it has to be worked out in the lifestyle of the believer. Life is a succession of moral choices, and the acceptance of the cross as a means of liberation from the self life leads on to a continual application of 'not-I-but-Christ' decisions in daily life. We confirm the principle with the pattern. I choose not to answer back. I choose to switch off the television to do something productive. I choose to stop day-dreaming and get on with study. I choose to set aside time to pray for that friend in a crisis situation.

Peter has a word on this topic, 'Therefore, since Christ suffered in his body, arm yourselves also with the same attitude' (1 Pet. 4:1). The Lord Jesus says 'If anyone would come after me, he must deny himself and take up his cross daily and follow me' (Luke 9:23).

4. *Provision for victory over Satan*
'Since the children share in flesh and blood, He Himself likewise also partook of the same that through death He might render powerless him who had the power of death, that is the devil' (Heb. 2:15 NASB).

Here then, is the fourth dimension of the cross as taught in the New Testament. Christ's death was not only a sacrifice for our sin – it was also God's method of breaking Satan's power in human life. Shortly expecting to die on the cross, Jesus made this amazing statement in John 12:31, 'Now the prince of this world will be driven out.' Jesus knew that his dying was to break Satan's power.

Just as everyone can come to God and receive forgiveness through faith in the cross-work of Christ, so every believer can claim victory over Satan by faith in the cross-work of Christ. Both stem from the cross! No matter what illusion of powerlessness Satan seeks to create we can stand firm in the knowledge that he is a defeated foe.

Summary

Dimension 1: Salvation – The *pardon* of the cross
Dimension 2: Liberation – The *principle* of the cross
Dimension 3: Discipline – The *pattern* of the cross
Dimension 4: Victory – The *power* of the cross

Further reading

Calvary Road, Roy Hession, Christian Literature Crusade

The Cross of Christ, F J Huegel, Bethany

Overcomers Through the Cross, Paul Billheimer, Christian Literature Crusade

The Cross of Calvary, Jessie Penn-Lewis

31 *Tips on Recognising and Resisting Satan*

Probably Satan's chief strategy is to lull God's people into the feeling that he doesn't even exist. In schools of liberal theology the concept of a personal devil is met with derision, but ask any missionary committed to evangelism, church planting and the releasing of people from the bondage of heathenism and you will hear a different story.

Recognising Satan

Here is a list of the activities ascribed to him in the New Testament:

1. Tempter. He connives to ensure we are tempted in a way that takes the greatest possible advantage of our character and situation. In the temptation of Christ his suggestion was that, since Christ was hungry yet had supernatural powers, he could turn stones into bread (Luke 4:4).

2. Liar and the father of lies. Jesus describes him as such in John 8:44. Satan is diametrically opposed to truth, so he will seek to twist it or contradict it to his own advantage. His first words through the serpent in the garden of Eden were to query the truth of God's spoken word: 'Did God really say . . .?' (Gen. 3:1).

3.   Murderer and devourer. He is implacably opposed to God's servants and has a firm purpose of destruction, in the spiritual, mental and even physical realm. 'The devil prowls around like a lion looking for someone to devour' (1 Pet. 5:8).

4.   Enemy. We are called upon to resist him as an enemy and to defend ourselves against him using the weapons provided. 'Put on the full armour of God so that you can take your stand against the devil's schemes' (Eph. 6:11).

5.   Accuser and slanderer. He is described in Revelation 12:10 as 'the accuser of our brothers'. His name *diabolos* means one who hurls things at people. He will seek to poison your mind by placing accusations in it regarding other people. And if he can't succeed in this he will probably try to accuse you to yourself, seeking to bring you under self-condemnation: 'I'm no good.' The Holy Spirit will bring conviction, leading to cleansing. Satan brings condemnation from which there is no relief (until we realise what is happening and resist him).

6.   Counterfeiter. Paul says in 2 Corinthians 11:14 that Satan himself 'masquerades as an angel of light.' It is not surprising then, if his servants masquerade as servants of righteousness. For example, several false cults emphasise doing 'good deeds' as a means of earning acceptance with God. Paul refers to Satan's 'counterfeit miracles, signs and wonders' in 2 Thessalonians 2:9.

7.   Hinderer. He will constantly strive to hinder committed Christians from carrying out God's revealed will. Paul says in 1 Thessalonians 2:18 that he wanted to come to visit the Thessalonians 'but Satan stopped us.' How does he do this? Perhaps by causing sickness, or discouragement, or stimulating a wrong attitude in another which hinders the accomplishment of God's plan. Once you have become convinced about God's will in a major area of your life (see pages 34 to 38), test very carefully the

sudden 'feeling' that God may be leading you off in a completely different direction.

8. Misleader. 1 Timothy 4:1 says that 'in later times some will abandon the faith and follow deceiving spirits and things taught by demons.' The Greek word for deceive means 'to lead off the track'. This can happen in matters of doctrine, but it can also happen in the area of God's leading in our lives.

9. Trickster. The phrase in Ephesians 6:11, 'the devil's schemes' uses the word *methodia* coming from *meta*, change, *hodos*, way, the idea being the creation of confusion by upsetting current plans.

10. Stimulator of lust. Ephesians 2:2, 3 says '. . . you followed the ways of this world and of the ruler of the kingdom of the air, the spirit who is now at work in those who are disobedient. All of us also lived among them at one time, gratifying the cravings of our sinful nature and following its desires and thoughts.' Satan is capable of stimulating perfectly normal desires into inflamed uncontrollable passions. We need to bring our desires daily under the control of the Spirit.

11. Ensnarer. 1 Timothy 3:7 talks about 'the devil's trap.' He seeks to create situations where there will be enormous pressure on the Christian to yield to a certain temptation. Witness the trap he laid for Joseph through the attentions of Potiphar's wife in Genesis 39:12.

12. Deceiver. He is a master at creating false impressions, spreading misunderstandings, and suggesting innuendos. He is described in Revelation 12:9 as someone 'who leads the whole world astray.'

13. Promoter of pride. He stimulates man's high estimation of himself. 'You will be like God . . .' (Gen. 3:5), but 'The Lord detests all the proud of heart' (Prov. 16:5).

14. Oppressor. Discouragement can lead to depression

and depression to oppression – all of them the work of the enemy. In Acts 10:38 the words 'all who were under the power of' comes from a Greek word meaning 'to exercise power over' or oppress. Of course, Satan uses 'normal' circumstances to influence the mind. Homesickness can lead to self-pity and depression. When the Christian worker sees people unresponsive to the gospel, Satan can use this to cause discouragement. The actual events do not provide the negative influence; it is Satan's use of these in our minds.

15. Troubler. Paul's testimony in 2 Corinthians 12:7 is that a certain physical problem that he had was 'a messenger of Satan', and Jesus cured many people by exorcising demons. However, not all sickness is satanic.

16. Blinder of men's minds. Since he is anti-truth (point 2) he works hard to hinder people from understanding the gospel. He is described in 2 Corinthians 4:4 as having 'blinded the minds of unbelievers, so that they cannot see the light of the gospel'. Hence the need for the Holy Spirit's ministry of enlightenment. He is called 'the Spirit of truth' (John 16:13).

17. Ruler of darkness. His kingdom, being totally void of truth, peace and love, is rightly called the kingdom of darkness. Paul's calling, as stated in Acts 26:18, was to turn the Gentiles 'from darkness to light, and from the power of Satan to God'.

18. Director of demonic activity. We are told that our struggle is against 'the powers of this dark world and against the spiritual forces of evil' (Eph. 6:12). This describes Satan and his demonic army.

19. Suppressor of the word of God. Jesus explains in the parable of the seeds and the weeds, 'The one who sowed the good seed is the Son of Man. The field is the world, and the good seed stands for the sons of the kingdom. The weeds are the sons of the evil one, and the enemy who sows them is the devil' (Matt. 13:37-39). In the

parable of the sower, Jesus explains that 'the seed is the word of God. Those along the path are the ones who hear, and then the devil comes and takes away the word from their hearts, so that they cannot believe and be saved' (Luke 8:11, 12).

20. Prince of this world. Just before the events leading up to Calvary, Jesus said to his disciples, 'Now is the time for judgment on this world; now the prince of this world will be driven out' (John 12:31).

21. Creator of division. Discussing his relationship with the Corinthian believers — which has not been a smooth one — Paul says 'What I have forgiven — if there was anything to forgive — I have forgiven in the sight of Christ for your sake, in order that Satan might not outwit us. For we are not unaware of his schemes' (2 Cor. 2:10, 11). In other words, 'Satan is out to stir up trouble between us and keep us estranged, but we're not going to let him get away with that.'

Resisting Satan

What is the ground of our ability to defeat Satan? Watchman Nee has said, 'Christianity is not a great big do. It's a great big done!' All that needs to be done to put us in the position of victors has been done. Every Christian needs to be absolutely clear about all the advantages and rights he possesses through faith in Christ's work at the cross.

22. We have been brought out of Satan's kingdom and into Christ's. 'For he has rescued us from the dominion of darkness and brought us into the kingdom of the Son he loves' (Col. 1:13). Paul goes even further and uses very bold absolute terms in Colossians 3:3, 'For you died, and your life is now hidden with Christ in God.' We don't have to struggle with Satan. We simply walk away because a gulf has come between us and him by our being brought into a faith-relationship to Christ.

23. Satan's power has been broken. Why is it that the saints are described in Revelation 12:11 as having overcome the devil 'by the blood of the Lamb and by the word of their testimony'? Because by dying, and rising from the dead, Christ broke Satan's power. Hebrews 2:14, 15 says, 'He too [Christ] shared in their humanity so that by his death he might destroy him who holds the power of death – that is, the devil'. 'Destroy' here does not mean 'annihilate' but 'render powerless'.

24. The advantages of the new relationship. As we assert total faith in this new position and relationship, we can claim all the advantages of being new people in Christ. As Paul says, 'If anyone is in Christ, he is a new creation; the old has gone, the new has come!' (2 Cor. 5:17). Nothing of the old life – habits, thought-patterns, values – need limit us in the new relationship. 'If the Son sets you free, you will be free indeed' (John 8:36).

25. The believer is super-conqueror – in Christ. Paul describes the position of Christians as being those who are literally 'super-conquerors' (Romans 8:37). In Romans 5 Paul has already stated that Christians are those who reign in life through one man, Jesus Christ. And in 1 Peter 2:9 we are given the title of 'a royal priesthood'.

26. Asserting our authority. The Lord Jesus taught very clearly that although Satan's power was to be broken at the cross, we would still have to assert our authority. 'No-one can enter a strong man's house and carry off his possessions unless he first ties up the strong man. Then he can rob his house' (Mark 3:27).

Defeating Satan

27. Submit unreservedly to God's will. James 4:7 states this as a prerequisite to resisting Satan: 'Submit yourselves, then, to God. Resist the devil, and he will flee from you.'

28. Resist him on the authority of your position in Christ. 'Resist him, standing firm in the faith' (1Peter 5:9). 'Do not give the devil a foothold' (Eph. 4:27).

29. Rely on the cross-work of Christ: 'Having disarmed the powers and authorities, he made a public spectacle of them, triumphing over them by the cross' (Col. 2:15).

30. Wear the full armour. Note these four references to standing in Ephesians 6:

'Put on the full armour of God so that you can take your stand against the devil's schemes' (verse 11).

'Put on the full armour of God, so that when the day of evil comes, you may be able to stand your ground, and after you have done everything, stand' (verse 13).

'Stand firm then . . .' (verse 14).

Note too the command to wear the full armour (verses 14-17). You need comprehensive not minimum cover!

31. Maintain a close vital relationship with the Lord. After the teaching on the Christian's armour in Ephesians 6, Paul gives us a pile-up of references to prayer. 'Pray in the Spirit on all occasions with all kinds of prayers and requests . . . Be alert and always keep on praying for all the saints. Pray also for me . . .' (verses 18, 19).

'They overcame him by the blood of the Lamb and by the word of their testimony' (Rev. 12:11).

Further reading

I Believe in Satan's Downfall, Michael Green, Hodder & Stoughton

Hidden Warfare, David Watson, STL Books

The Christian Soldier, D M Lloyd-Jones, Banner of Truth

War on the Saints, Jessie Penn Lewis, Overcomer Literature Trust

Destined for the Throne, Paul Billheimer, Christian Literature Crusade

12 Areas of Deliverance That Every Disciple Should Know

1. Freedom from condemnation

As a child of God you already know freedom from the guilt of past sin. But often Satan (who is the accuser) seeks to bring a sense of condemnation over failure. We have to realise that while the Holy Spirit convicts he never condemns. The Spirit's conviction leads us to the blood for cleansing; Satan's tactic is to put us in a morass of hopelessness; but 'there is no condemnation for those who are in Christ Jesus' (Rom. 8:1).

2. Freedom from the power of sin

Freedom from guilt is one thing; freedom from the power of sin is another. When we grasp this we are in a position of being able to choose not to sin. We can never know this experience on our own, but in Christ we are already delivered. The world says, 'Prove it and I'll believe it.' God says, 'Believe it and I'll prove it.' Romans 6 teaches that we have died to the power of sin.

We have come up in a new relationship – one with Christ in his risen life. We need to accept this truth in our mind, assert it in our spirit by faith, and apply it with the will in the situation saying, 'I refuse this (sin) on the ground of my new relationship with Christ and the brokenness of the old relationship to the power of sin'. As Paul puts it in Romans 6:11; 'Count yourselves dead to sin but alive to God in Christ Jesus.'

3.   Freedom from law

Any external pressure upon us to conform to a standard or pattern of behaviour is law. Law is not 'bad' – but it is not the basis of the Christian's holiness, because 'Christ is the end of the law so that there may be righteousness for everyone who believes' (Rom. 10:4). The law can only appeal to my self-effort, never to Christ in me. The Christian's motivation should arise from his inner union with Christ and the desire to please him, in his strength alone. Just as Romans 6 teaches that we have, in Christ, died to our sin, so Romans 7 teaches we have died to the law. When we do anything out of a sense of duty or conformity to a pattern or standard we are under law. Under law we are trying to do something for God. Under grace, God is doing something through us.

4.   Freedom from independent self

Independent self is called 'the flesh' in Scripture. There is only one satisfactory way to live the Christian life and that is in union with Christ. Colossians 2:6 says, 'Since you have accepted Christ Jesus as Lord, live in union with him' (TEV). Romans 8:2 says, 'For the law of the Spirit which brings us life in union with Christ Jesus, has set me free from the law of sin and death' (TEV). Our destiny is to be a container of the divine life. Anything we do which is not an expression of his life is flesh. The fleshly Christian lives in a twilight zone. He is in the kingdom, but described as an 'infant' in 1 Corinthians 3:1. Maturity is life under the control of the Spirit. Have we placed ourselves unreservedly under the lordship of Christ, for his will to be done in our lives? If not, life 'in the Spirit' is an impossibility.

5.   Freedom from the world

The world-system is based on human desires – the strong

desire of self (independence), the strong desire to have what our eyes can see (materialism), the strong desire for acclaim (pride). Paul says (and we need to come to the same conviction and commitment), 'May I never boast except in the cross of our Lord Jesus Christ, through which the world has been crucified to me, and I to the world' (Gal. 6:14). Whenever our motivation comes from self-seeking, materialistic gain, desire for recognition or the assertion of our so-called 'rights' we are keeping company with the world system.

6. Freedom from Satan and evil spirits
The conflict with satanic powers is a real one. Disciples need to understand that they share Christ's position of authority over them. Not only do we share Christ's resurrection life, we read in Ephesians 2:6 that we share his ascended position – his place of vantage and authority over satanic forces. 'The reason the Son of God appeared was to destroy the devil's work' (1 John 3:8). Jesus said to his disciples: 'If I drive out demons by the Spirit of God, then the kingdom of God has come upon you . . . how can anyone enter a strong man's house and carry off his possessions unless he first ties up the strong man?' (Matt. 12:28, 29).

7. Freedom from fear
Romans 8:15 tells us that we, as children of God, have received the spirit of Sonship not the spirit of fear. Paul tells Timothy that he has not been given the spirit of fear but of 'power, of love and of self-discipline' (2 Tim. 1:7). This does not mean that we will never be 'afraid'. If we didn't 'fear' the approach of a fast car we would not jump out of the way. But the Bible is talking about a crippling spirit of fearfulness. Fortunately we are given the divine antidote – love. 'Perfect love drives out fear' (1 John 4:18). So when we allow divine love to capture our hearts – and remember 'God has poured out his love into our hearts' (Rom. 5:5) – then fear simply flees. 'There is no fear in love' (1 John 4:18).

8. Freedom from unbelief

It is often a surprise for a Christian to realise that unbelief is not 'sitting on the fence'; it is a conscious or even unconscious refusal to exercise faith. Hebrews 3:12 says, 'See to it, brothers, that none of you has a sinful, unbelieving heart'. The word for sinful implies 'positively evil'. Failure to have faith is really moving in diametric opposition to the purposes of God. Faith is an issue of the will, and the human heart is capable of responding to the scriptural command, 'Stop doubting and believe' (John 20:27).

9. Freedom from the fleshly mind

The fleshly mind is the mind dominated by human rationalism. It is opposed to the spiritual mind. The two are differentiated in Romans 8:4-8. It is quite possible to be a Christian and still have a fleshly mind. 1 Corinthians 3:1-3 makes this clear; Paul is speaking to Christians who have never 'grown up'. How is the spiritual mind cultivated? By exposing the understanding to spiritual truth and submitting the spirit to the lordship of Christ. This is usually a crisis of 'brokenness', followed by a process of continuous submission.

10. Freedom from a critical spirit

God gives Christians discernment, but often Satan seeks to turn this gift into a curse by injecting it with a judgmental spirit. This is specifically forbidden by Jesus in Matthew 7:1-5. One of Satan's names is the 'accuser'. When we become judgmental and condemnatory we are doing Satan's work for him. Even when another is known to have failed, Galatians 6:1 instructs us to take steps to gently restore him.

11. Freedom from depression and despair

Jesus said that his 'meat' (the thing that satisfied him) was doing the Father's will (John 4:34.) Depression is often the result of disobedience. How can hope be stimulated? We learn from Romans 5:3-5 that pressure is meant to produce perseverance. Perseverance produces character and this produces hope. All this is possible because the love of God has been shed abroad in our hearts. Psalms 42 and 43 stress that hope and praise are the keys to release.

12. Freedom from sensuality and lust

Every Christian has normal bodily appetites. Their satisfaction in God's time and way bring delight and fulfilment but when they are permitted to overpower our inner centre of control – the spirit – we move along a road on which their cravings become more intense and more demanding. The secret is threefold: accept in the mind the truth of being already liberated from the old unregenerate you with its passions and lusts (2 Corinthians 5:17). Assert this truth in your spirit as a deliberate act of faith ('you have taken off your old self' Col. 3:9) and apply the truth of your new indwelling relationship, with your will, moving positively in the line of obedience ('put on the new self' Col. 3:10).

Further reading

Defeated Enemies, Corrie ten Boom, Christian Literature Crusade

Fullness and Freedom, Dick Lucas, Inter-Varsity Press

The Fight, John White, Inter-Varsity Press

Flirting with the World, John White, STL Books

From Now On, Ralph Shallis, STL Books

Into Action, Charles Marsh, STL Books

10 *Steps to Christian Freedom*

It is absolutely imperative for every disciple to understand the liberating truths taught in Romans 6.

1. This chapter expounds a key spiritual truth for the disciple – namely his release from the domination of Satan through his union with Christ, and the possibility of victory on the basis of this new relationship. The same truths come through in other passages, such as 2 Corinthians 5:17: 'If anyone is in Christ, he is a new creation; the old has gone . . .'; Philippians 3:10: 'I want to know Christ and the power of his resurrection and the fellowship of sharing in his sufferings, becoming like him in his death'; 1 Peter 2:24: 'He himself bore our sins in his body on the tree, so that we might die to sins and live for righteousness.'

2. It is essential to see the purpose of the two parts of this chapter. In verses 1-11 Paul addresses the Christian's mind. The key words are 'know' (vv. 3, 6, 9); 'believe' (v. 8); 'count' (v. 11). So the appeal is to the spiritual understanding, that it may grasp the significance of the new relationship. In verses 12-23 he addresses the will, the key words being 'offer' (vv. 16, 19), 'obey' (v. 16), 'slaves' (vv. 16-20, 22). The appeal is to assert the power of the new

relationship and bring our lives in line with what Christ wants.

3. Paul uses the term death or die fourteen times in verses 1-11. It is important to understand the significance of this. 'Death' in Scripture never means 'annihilation' but 'separation'. The Greek work is *apothnesko*; *apo* is a prefix meaning 'from'. So Paul is saying, 'You died out to the old relationship to sin' which is treated here as a power or force, behind which is the person of Satan.

4. Verses 3, 4 and 5 contain imagery to strengthen the force of the argument that we have 'died out' to this old relationship. Baptism here is not physical baptism (just as burial in verse 4 is not physical burial). The word means 'to immerse'. So the person we used to be has been immersed or placed into Christ's death. Paul then says the 'old self' has been entombed with Christ (v. 3), fused together in his death (v. 4), and in verse 6 he says we have been crucified together with Christ. The three Greek verbs used all carry a prefix which means 'along with' – *sunthapto, sumphuo* and *sustauroo* – graphic words that display the break with sin which every new believer can and should experience.

5. Verse 6 contains phrases which are easily misunderstood. The 'old self' is the person you used to be, outside of Christ. The 'body of sin' can best be interpreted as 'the body which has been the vehicle of sin'. So the verse means, 'The person we used to be was crucified together with Christ so that the body which has been the vehicle of sin may be idle as far as sin is concerned.'

6. Verse 7 says that he who has died to sin has been freed from sin. This does not mean that we cannot be tempted; but it does mean that we have the privilege of living beyond its claim. (The word used for free, *dikaioo* carries the sense that Christ's death annulled all obligations – satisfied all penalties, and the Christian's identification with Christ takes him beyond sin's claim. Further subservience to it need not take place.

7. The fact of Christ's death to sin is the ground of the Christian's freedom. The final picture in this section is an

analogy drawn from the 'once-for-all' nature of Christ's death. He paid the penalty for sin and satisfied the demand that sin made totally and completely in one act of dying. Now he lives for God. The Christian is to count it a fact that he too had died to the demand of sin and has come alive through Christ. Hence he has no need to go on living in sin.

8. This freedom can now be experienced in practical living. Verses 12 to 23 constitute an appeal to the will to assert its freedom, by

- Refusing to allow sin any authority (vv. 12, 13).
- Presenting ourselves positively to God as instruments of righteousness (v. 13).
- Obeying the form of teaching to which we have committed ourselves (in becoming Christians) (v. 17).

9. The will is depicted as free and capable of producing a life of holiness. Formerly, as heathen, the Romans had applied their wills to a life of sin, leading to spiritual death, but now they were in a position to apply their wills to a life of holiness (v. 19), the final outcome of which is eternal life (vv. 22, 23).

10. A common question about this chapter is: 'I don't feel dead to sin. How can it be true?' All of us can be responsive to temptation until we die. 'Dead' doesn't mean 'impervious' but it does mean that I can exercise faith in the new relationship and stand on the fact that the old relationship has been broken. I am thus capable of resisting temptation and of going God's way (1 Cor. 10:13).

Further reading

The Normal Christian Life, Watchman Nee, Kingsway
Born Crucified, L E Maxwell, Moody Press
Bone of His Bone, F J Huegel, Zondervan

22 *Guidelines on How To Understand and Develop Faith*

1. Living by faith is normal

The Christian life commences with an act of faith in which, having repented of sin, we accept Christ as our Saviour. Colossians 2:5, 6 says, 'I . . . delight to see . . . how firm your faith in Christ is. So then, just as you received Christ Jesus as Lord, continue to live in him, rooted and built up in him, strengthened in the faith'. The clear implication is that as faith brings us into union with Christ, so faith maintains the union. We cannot maintain spiritual life by any other means than by faith.

2. Faith is scriptural

Hebrews 11:6 says, 'Without faith it is impossible to please God'. Romans 5:1 says, 'Since we have been justified through faith, we have peace with God through our Lord Jesus Christ, through whom we have gained access by faith into this grace in which we now stand.' Galatians 3:11 says, 'The righteous will live by faith.' The whole book of Galatians warns us against thinking that we can replace faith with anything of our own merit. The life of salvation is on the ground of faith alone.

3. The alternative to faith is self-reliance

When we try to live the Christian life in our own strength,

out of vital union with Christ, we are described as being fleshly. We are in the twilight zone, knowing forgiveness, yet not living a life of total reliance on Christ. In other words we are living by our own human resources. Paul says to the Corinthian church members, 'I could not address you as spiritual but as worldly – mere infants in Christ' (1 Cor. 3:1).

Understand the three levels of faith

4. *Claiming faith (level one)*
Three levels of faith are seen in Scripture. Claiming faith is simply accepting what God offers us. It is 'kindergarten' faith, requiring nothing more than comprehending what God is offering, and taking it. For instance, when we accept Christ's invitation to 'Come unto me', we are responding with claiming faith. 'To all who received him, to those who believed in his name, he gave the right to become children of God' (John 1:12).

5. *Creative faith (level two)*
As we grow in Christ and become involved in his purposes, we will be challenged to trust God to work in people's lives, to change situations, to provide spiritual strength or material supply. This active trust is always on the basis of his revealed will, but it will call forth a deliberate commitment of faith on our part. For instance, when the woman with a haemorrhage came and touched Christ in the crowd, Jesus said, 'Your faith has healed you' (Luke 8:44-48). When Peter was told to come to Christ across the water he was able to do so as long as he walked by faith (Matthew 14:29).

6. *Conquering faith (level three)*
Christians are engaged in a spiritual warfare and we can resist Satan only on the basis of faith in the finished work of Christ. Jesus defeated Satan on the cross and in the resurrection, but believers have to assert that victory by faith. We overcome 'by the blood of the Lamb' (Rev.

12:11), and we can resist satanic onslaught with the shield of faith (Ephesians 6:16). 'This is the victory that has overcome the world, even our faith' (1 John 5:4).

Understand the practical aspects of faith

7. A knowledge of God's purpose is essential for faith to operate

We cannot exert faith for a particular goal unless we are sure that it is in God's purpose. Hence the disciple is called to live a life of sensitivity so that he can discern God's will. This is what is meant in 1 Corinthians 2:15 where it talks about the spiritual man having discernment. This issue of knowing takes time: it requires reflection, prayer and meditation. Often discussion with other Christians helps to clarify and solidify a conviction. The final indicator is the peace of the Lord reigning in our hearts. This peace is given by the Holy Spirit. Colossians 3:15 says, 'Let the peace of Christ rule in your hearts'.

8. The experience of faith

The reality of faith is evidenced by practical steps taken on the conviction that our ultimate faith-goal will be achieved. When we buy a ticket to go on a plane we act in faith regarding the plane's airworthiness, the ability of the pilot and his intention of flying the plane to our destination. When we believe that God means to work in a situation we must begin to take the practical steps necessary towards this, even without outward guarantees about the rightness of the goal. Commitment is the key. In Luke 5:5 Peter took his boat out and let down the net by faith. 'Because you say so, I will let down the nets.'

9. Knowing God's promises is essential for faith

Faith is a response to the promises of God. For instance, James 4:6, 7 says that if we submit ourselves to God and resist the devil he will flee from us; it is our responsibility to ensure we are fulfilling the condition (submission) and then to resist Satan in the confidence that he must depart.

So we need to know the promises so that we can put a faith-claim upon them.

10. Faith and prayer
Prayer in itself does not move the hand of God. Prayer is often a means of bringing us out of unbelief into faith. Mark 11:24 says, 'whatever you ask for in prayer, believe that you have received it'. Prayer is meant to bring us to faith. God's word says, 'According to your faith will it be done to you' (Matt. 9:29).

11. Faith and praise
The evidence of having reached a place of faith is a praiseful spirit. The disciple no longer asks, he expects and rejoices in anticipation of the answer. When we can thank God because we 'see' the invisible as visible – that is faith. See Romans 4:20 where it says of Abraham, regarding having a son, that he was strong in faith and 'gave glory to God'.

12. Faith and declaration
When we do reach a place of faith-and-praise, it would appear from Scripture that it pleases the heart of God when we declare our faith either by word or act. When Moses was praying about the Israelites crossing the Red Sea, God said, 'Why are you crying out to me? Tell the Israelites to move on' (Exod. 14:15).

13. Tests of faith
God will allow our faith to be tested. The answer may not come at the time we think it should or in the way we expect. There is an element of importunity or persistence about faith. We have to hold on, and stay positive in our expectancy. In Luke 11:1-13 the needy neighbour gets what he wants by shameless persistence.

How can we have more faith?

14. Scripture says, 'Ask and it will be given to you; seek and you will find' (Luke 11:9). So the simplest answer

to that question is, 'Ask God for more faith.' The disciples said, 'Lord, increase our faith' (Luke 17:5).

15. Our faith will be strengthened if we familiarise ourselves with the lives of men and women of faith down through history to the present day – from the 'heroes of faith' in Hebrews 11 to Hudson Taylor and C T Studd.

16. The word says, 'Faith comes from hearing the message, and the message is heard through the word of Christ' (Rom. 10:17). So – study the word. Use a concordance. Look up references to 'faith', 'believe', 'trust', and complete your own theology of faith.

17. Use the faith you have. Jesus likened faith to a grain of mustard seed – a tiny seed, yet capable of enormous growth. Little faith has the potential of becoming great faith, if you exercise what you already have. 'I do believe; help me overcome my unbelief' (Mark 9:24).

What hinders faith?

18. Unconfessed sin
Faith is inhibited when sin remains unconfessed. Psalm 66:18 says, 'If I had cherished sin in my heart, the Lord would not have listened'.

19. Continuing sinful acts or attitudes
The Scriptures warn us about having:

- A critical spirit (Matthew 7:1-5).
- An unforgiving spirit (Mark 11:25).
- Pride (James 4:6).
- A spirit of anger (Ephesians 4:26, 27).
- A root of bitterness (Hebrews 12:15).
- Dislike or hatred (1 John 2:9-11).
- A spirit of fear (2 Timothy 1:7).
- Jealousy (Proverbs 6:34; 27:4).

'If we confess our sins [specific acts or attitudes] ,he is faithful and just and will forgive us our sins and purify us from all unrighteousness' (1 John 1:9).

20. Unbelief

Hebrews 3:12 describes the 'sinful, unbelieving heart' which seeks to turn us away from positive faith in God. Satan is always present to cast doubt on the word of God. Look at Genesis 3:1. The serpent asks, 'Did God really say . . .?' Disciples need to recognise and resist unbelief as a satanic counterattack on faith.

What is the difference between faith as a fruit and faith as a gift of the Spirit?

21. The spiritual fruit of faith mentioned in Galatians 5:22 is best translated as 'faithfulness'. It is the capacity to continue with a simple basic reliance in the Lord and his word, and to live a life that is consistent with that faith. By so doing we become 'faith-ful'.

22. The gift of faith in 1 Corinthians 12:9 is a specific enabling of the Spirit given to some to discern God's purpose in an unusually clear way and to maintain a confident stance of expectancy and trust for its accomplishment, co-operating with God in taking practical steps of trust as he leads. George Muller had this gift and was able to trust God for all the material necessities of a large orphanage without making these needs known. One night he realised there was no food for the next morning's breakfast but he confidently committed it to the Lord in faith and went to sleep. During the night a Christian baker was led to bake an extra batch of rolls and to send them to the orphanage in time for breakfast in the morning.

Further reading

George Muller: Delighted in God, Roger Steer, STL Books

Faith for the Future, Colin Urquhart, Hodder & Stoughton

A Living Faith, Helen Roseveare, Hodder & Stoughton

Mighty Faith, J Oswald Sanders, Moody

28 *Questions To Ask About That Relationship*

After the issues of conversion and commitment to the lordship of Christ no issue has a greater impact on life than the decision regarding one's life partner. It has the potential for immeasurable enrichment or for spiritual shipwreck.

1. Are you both approaching this subject responsibly, recognising it as a serious issue of obedience and discipleship, and not just as a pleasurable emotional experience?

2. Do you have an overall sense of harmony and compatibility with the person you are considering as a life partner? 'Can two walk together except they be agreed?' (Amos 3:3 AV). To walk successfully through life with another person large areas of agreement must exist from the outset, with plenty of room for adjustment as time goes on.

3. Is there compatibility in temperament? God makes no two persons the same, but he does make temperaments that fit. For example, if one party is slow, deliberate, painstaking and the other is mercurial, careless and given to quick decisions that lack careful thought, beware.

4. In matters of the mind, do you relate well and is there an ease in 'latching on' to each other's ideas? Frustration is inevitable if one party has a significant intellectual advantage over the other.

The most important area in the consideration of compatibility is the spiritual. Consider these aspects:

5. Do you have similar interests when it comes to spiritual matters?

6. Do you have a similar intensity of interest in spiritual things? For instance, is Bible reading a delight to one party and a drag to the other?

7. Are you a stimulus to one another in Christian faith and action? Hebrews 10:24 says; 'Let us consider how we may spur one another on towards love and good deeds.'

8. Do you find it easy and natural to pray together?

9. Are you each evidencing a serious concern to discover God's will for your lives?

10. Do you evidence such skills and spiritual gifts that will enable you to complement each other and make you a balanced team in serving the Lord?

11. Do you agree on such basic matters of doctrine as the inspiration of Scripture, deity of Christ, salvation through faith in Christ's atoning work?

12. Do you agree on other matters of doctrine such as the place of the Holy Spirit in the life of the believer and what constitutes a 'church'?

13. Do you have a clear understanding about what the Scriptures say about the responsibility of the husband to the wife, and the wife to the husband? (Study Ephesians 5:22-28; 1 Corinthians 7:1-6; 1 Peter 3:1-7.)

Here are some other vital questions for the compatibility test:

14. Is there compatibility in age? Generally speaking minimal adjustments are needed if one partner is within five years of the other, and both are under thirty.

15.   Is there compatibility in social and personal interests, for example, music, politics, sport, etc.?

16.   Is there agreement on moral standards (e.g. sex, keeping promises, honesty and openness)?

17.   Is there compatibility in the level of self-discipline, for example, regarding food, sleep, restraint in physical intimacy?

18.   Is there an ease in each other's company with a freedom for each to express ideas and concepts without feeling inhibited?

19.   Is each free in the social circle of the other?

20.   Do you have an agreed understanding on family planning?

21.   Is there an agreement on how you are going to solve the problem of 'competing claims' in your life once you are married? For example, work, service, church, family.

As the true essence of love is giving rather than getting, it is worthwhile considering these points:

22.   What is uppermost when you meet – self-giving or self-gratification? '[Love] is not self-seeking' (1 Cor. 13:5).

23.   Do you accept the scriptural injunction regarding serving one another? 'Serve one another in love,' (Gal. 5:13).

24.   Are you capable of anticipating one another's emotional needs?

25.   Are you thoughtful for each other's physical condition. For example, sufficient sleep, adequate food and rest?

Finally, consider these all important issues:

26.   Is your walk with the Lord being enriched or enfeebled by this friendship?

27.   Is the Holy Spirit giving you a strong, lasting inner conviction about the rightness of it? 'Let the peace of Christ rule [be the umpire] in your hearts' (Col. 3:15).

28.   Is your supreme motive in this issue the will of God?

'My food . . . is to do the will of him who sent me' (John 4:34).

Further reading

Eros Defiled, John White, Inter-Varsity Press
Givers, Takers and Other Kinds of Lovers, Josh McDowell, Kingsway
The Christian Couple, L & N Christenson, Kingsway
Growing Into Love, Joyce Huggett, Inter-Varsity Press
Love Is a Feeling To Be Learned, Walter Trobisch, Inter-Varsity Press
Man to Man About Women, James Dobson, Kingsway
Marriage As God Intended, Selwyn Hughes, Kingsway

25 *Considerations When Preparing for Christian Service*

It's one thing to stand up or come forward at a meeting, indicating surrender to the lordship of Christ and a willingness to be open regarding the possibility of full time Christian service. It's another thing to follow this up with the sort of steps that the nature of this commitment requires, namely a re-aligning of one's life so as to be prepared to respond to God's call to full time service if and when it comes. The following points are briefly listed as a help to those who want to be ready:

Your lifestyle – a personal challenge

1. Adopt a disciple's lifestyle. This means action on four fronts – regular prayer, study of the word, fellowship with others who are likeminded, and witness to the unconverted. The basis of becoming an effective Christian worker is a life of balance and self-discipline.

2. Maintain a close walk with the Lord. Learn the experience taught in John 15, about cultivating a vital relationship with Christ, and you will become sensitive to the leading of the Holy Spirit. 'If a man remains in me and I in him, he will bear much fruit' (John 15:5).

3. Bring the issue of knowing God's will daily to the

Lord, in faith, asserting your confidence that he does and will guide. 'I will instruct you and teach you in the way you should go' (Ps. 32:8).

Your church – a sphere of service

4. Make yourself available for service in your local church. If you are not a member, join it officially. Discuss this with your pastor so that he is aware of your commitment.

5. If possible try to find an avenue of service which involves teaching on a regular basis. This will make you learn and give you contact with people. Attend training classes if they are available.

6. In your participation in church activities look out for one in which you have a sense of fulfilment. This could possibly indicate your spiritual gift, and this in turn could give direction regarding future service. (See page 81 for development of this idea.)

7. If no sphere of service opens up in your local church it may be that you are meant to work with an interdenominational group such as Open Air Campaigners, Navigators, ISCF, Youth for Christ, etc.

Your potential – an area for development

8. If these experiences of service give you an increasing conviction that you will go into full-time Christian work in the future, consider the possibility of doing a correspondence course with a Bible college as a first step.

9. Read the biographies of men and women who have been greatly used of God. Note the way God guided them, and the various forms of preparation into which God led them.

10. If you are in the midst of training for a secular profession or trade, complete it.

11. Institute a serious plan for saving, so that you have money on hand for your training, if the Lord so leads.

Your future – assess the alternatives

12.   Ask God to clarify whether your future lies in denominational service or in interdenominational work. Seek guidance from your pastor and other spiritually-minded friends regarding how best to prepare.

13.   If thinking of work with a denomination the normal procedure is to train at its own theological college, after fulfilling entrance qualifications.

14.   If you are heading for interdenominational service you should consider attending a Bible college or Missionary Training Centre. Write and obtain a prospectus. (See page 109 on Bible college training.)

15.   Seek information about the various forms of service available. For example, 'career' missionary, short-term worker (usually one or two years), or a professional worker overseas – university lecturer, rural development officer, civil engineer, etc.

16.   If you know your future lies with an overseas missionary organisation seek to become familiar with the principles and practice of some of them – and the qualifications they expect from applicants. Ask God to lay the mission of his choice on your heart, and trust him to give you personal contact with some of its workers. Attend its conferences and prayer groups.

17.   Several organisations sponsor short, or very short-term service. These include Teen Missions, Operation Mobilisation, and Youth With A Mission. These give good insights into overseas work and valuable experience. Membership is usually possible without Bible college training because some basic training is given prior to active service.

Some often-asked questions

18.   What kinds of Missions are there?

(a)   Short-term missions such as OM and YWAM which give basic training and experience in evangelism.

(b) Evangelistic and church-planting missions, such as OMF, WEC, SIM, SUM and many others.

(c) Service agencies such as Gospel Recordings, Bible Societies, and the Leprosy Mission.

(d) Specialist ministries such as Wycliffe Bible Translators (Linguistics), Trans World Radio, Far East Broadcasting Commission (Radio), Gospel Literature Outreach, Christian Literature Crusade (Literature), Missionary Aviation Fellowship (Aviation), Child Evangelism Fellowship (Children). Some of these also function as service missions.

(e) Relief agencies (World Vision, TEAR Fund, HEED).

19. What do Missions require by way of Bible Training? Most societies require a minimum of two years full-time residential Bible training.

20. If I have finished school and have missions in mind what sort of secular training would be good first?

(a) Obtain a qualification for an occupation useful in missions, such as a teacher, nurse, builder, electronic engineer, artist, journalist or secretary.

(b) Take a university course in Linguistics and Anthropology or Sociology.

(c) If you are working for a commercial firm take part-time studies in business administration and management.

21. If I have some time to 'fill in' before Bible training what sort of job should I try to get?

A job that enables you to have a high level of interaction with people, e.g. sales assistant, receptionist, labourer, or door-to-door salesman.

22. How long should I have been a Christian before going into Bible training?

At least a year should elapse after your conversion – a year in which you should be growing spiritually, and actively serving the Lord.

23. What should I have done before Bible training?

• Helped effectively in church work. (Your pastor will

be asked for a reference on your character and
service.)
- Read the Bible through (and know the books off by
heart!)
- Lead someone to Christ.

24. We are married with two children. Is there a
possibility of us going to the mission field? Yes, but a lot
depends on your background and experience. You will
both require Bible training. A number of colleges have
facilities for families. Another important issue is the
education of the children. Quite a number of missions have
schools for missionaries' children on the field but these do
not usually go beyond high school level.

25. Have you any final advice to a future Christian
worker? Yes. It cannot be too strongly emphasised that
being a missionary or Christian worker is not a task for a
'loner'. A missionary needs a support group which will
provide prayer backing. Missionary work is spiritual
warfare. So start praying now about your prayer-support
group. It may consist of members of your own local
church (you should certainly be identifying with it). It
maybe a circle wider than your church friends. But even
now, start by asking some to pray that you will know
God's will and have grace and determination to go through
with it.

Further reading

Into Action, Charles Marsh, STL Books
Missionary Without Pretending, Anne Townsend,
    Scripture Union
We Believe in Mission, John Wallis (ed.), STL Books
Don't Soft-pedal God's Call, Michael Griffiths, OMF
    Books
Going Places, Elizabeth Goldsmith, STL Books
Hunger for Reality, George Verwer, STL Books

22 Spiritual Gifts Defined and
8 Steps for Discovering Yours

Communication gifts

1. Teaching (Romans 12:7; 1 Corinthians 12:28; Ephesians 4:11.)
Teaching is the ability to explain and communicate biblical truth effectively so that those being taught receive spiritual enlightenment and understanding.

2. Encouraging (exhortation) (Romans 12:8.)
This is the ability to stimulate the will of others through the application of spiritual truth so that they are strengthened in their resolve to pursue God's will.

3. Prophecy (Romans 12:6; 1 Corinthians 12:10; 1 Corinthians 12:28; Ephesians 4:11.)
This is the effective telling forth of scriptural truth with particular relevance to a situation.

4. Message of wisdom (1 Corinthians 12:8.)
This is the ability to make a contribution to a situation which gives wise insights to those involved regarding the right course of action to pursue or decision to be made.

5. Message of knowledge (1 Corinthians 12:8.)
This is the gift of injecting into a given situation a

particular aspect of truth or factual knowledge that is highly relevant to the formulation of a correct decision.

6. *Speaking (1 Peter 4:11.)*
This is the communication of spiritual truth which can take place in a variety of situations.

7. *Evangelism (Ephesians 4:11.)*
This is the gift of being able to convey the gospel to the unsaved with such clarity and power that those hearing it are moved to respond to the claims of Christ.

8. *Tongues (1 Corinthians 12:10, 28; 14:1-27.)*
This is the ability either to worship God in an unknown language, or to pass on a message from God by specific inspiration, i.e. without consciously determining the form of expression.

9. *Interpretation of tongues (1 Corinthians 12:10; 14:27, 28.)*
This is the ability to re-express a message given through a tongues-speaker in the language of the hearers, without having a rational knowledge of the language in which the message was given.

Administration gifts

10. *Helping (1 Corinthians 12:28.)*
This gift is the special ability given to assist another in the task being accomplished. It involves perception and empathy and results in service which greatly enhances the effectiveness of the person helped.

11. *Contributing (Romans 12:8.)*
This is a gift involving sensitivity to the Lord and insight into the needs of God's work, resulting in a special ministry of giving so that the material needs of Christian work and workers are met.

12. *Leading (Romans 12:8.)*
This is the ability to discern God's will for a group, to

provide the initiative, and to handle the group with such wisdom and concern that all move forward in harmony to the agreed objective.

13. Showing mercy (Romans 12:8.)
This is the ability to sympathise readily with persons in special need and to become involved in a practical way in supporting them and alleviating their distress.

14. Faith (1 Corinthians 12:9.)
This is the ability to discern God's purposes, and to exercise positive trust and expectancy in him until the particular objective of faith is accomplished.

15. Serving (Romans 12:7; 1 Peter 4:11.)
This is the ability to discern practical needs and to give service so that the work of God is provided for in all its practical aspects.

16. Pastoring (Ephesians 4:11.)
This is the personal ministry of caring for people's spiritual welfare. It involves providing spiritual nourishment, protection, fellowship, prayer and counsel as needed.

17. Apostle (missionary) (1 Corinthians 12:28; Ephesians 4:11.)
Although in New Testament times this word had a special meaning, today it just carries the straight meaning of the original Greek word – 'sent one'. Some feel the word refers to missionaries – those who have a special ability in communicating the gospel over cultural and linguistic barriers. Others feel it is a term that should be reserved for mature spiritual leaders who have an itinerant ministry to churches, specialising in teaching and 'trouble-shooting'.

18. Hospitality (1 Peter 4:9.)
This is the gift of keeping your home open to visitors so that those who come sense its warmth and appreciate the atmosphere and fellowship given.

19. Administration (government) (1 Corinthians 12:28.)
This gift is the ability to organise and manage resources

(men, money, materials) so that all work together
smoothly for the accomplishment of group objectives.

Demonstration gifts

20. Healing (1 Corinthians 12:9.)
This gift involves the ability to consistently trust God to
bring about a cure for sickness. It is good to recognise
God's sovereignty in the time factor (not all healings are
instantaneous), and in the means factor (God can work by
miracle, or medicine, or both).

21. Distinguishing spirits (1 Corinthians 12:10.)
This is the ability to recognise the presence of an evil spirit,
even if that spirit is giving a semblance of being sent from
God. (See 1 John 4:1-3 on testing spirits.)

22. Miraculous power (1 Corinthians 12:10.)
This unusual gift has been exercised particularly effectively
in missionary situations when Christians are opposed by
strong satanic forces. It involves being able to trust God
for his intervention in a way that cannot be explained in
terms of natural phenomena.

8 steps for discovering your spiritual gift

1.   Accept the truth of 1 Peter 4:10 and 1 Corinthians
12:7 that every Christian has a spiritual gift, and thank
God for what he has given you. 'As each one has received a
special gift, employ it in serving one another' (1 Pet. 4:10
NASB). 'Now to each one the manifestation of the Spirit is
given for the common good' (1 Cor. 12:7).

2.   It is essential for a disciple to be committed to a
local fellowship. Hebrews 10:25 says, 'Let us not give up
meeting together'. This commitment provides the
groundwork for discovering one's gift because the purpose
of spiritual gifts is to edify the body (1 Corinthians
12:7-12). If we are not a vital part of a local fellowship we
have no God-given sphere in which to develop and exercise
a gift.

3. Commitment implies involvement. By being willing to undertake any aspect of service in the local fellowship we are starting on the road of discovery-by-experimentation as regards our gift or gifts.

4. Make this whole area a matter for specific believing prayer. Ask God to reveal his gift to you.

5. As you engage in various activities you will find a certain one or certain ones in which you will have a special sense of fulfilment and joy.

6. It is almost inevitable that the activities that give you fulfilment and joy will be the ones in which you are most effective. Expect to find evidence of effectiveness and success in your gift-activity.

7. It is wise to listen to others. Take note of their evaluation of your gifts, and make special note when other people consistently request your help along a particular line of service. They probably recognise your emerging gift.

8. Gifts seldom emerge 'overnight'. Usually it takes a considerable time for a gift to develop. If you are a new Christian (converted for less than eighteen months or even two years), do not make this a matter of anxiety and over-concern. So while point four emphasises the note of expectancy this needs to be balanced by the note of patience.

Further reading

Spiritual Gifts and the Church, Bridge & Phypers, Inter-Varsity Press

I Believe in the Holy Spirit, Michael Green, Hodder & Stoughton

The Holy Spirit and His Gifts, J Oswald Sanders, Zondervan

Cinderella's Betrothal Gifts, Michael Griffiths, OMF Books

How Much More?, Robert Gordon, Marshalls

Spirit Life, Stuart Briscoe, Kingsway

21 *Factors That Foster Fellowship*

'How good and pleasant it is when brothers live together in unity . . . there the Lord bestows his blessing . . .' (Ps. 133:1, 3). It is because of this truth that Satan constantly seeks to destroy unity. Fellowship needs to be worked at. It doesn't just happen. Scripture teaches the need to observe these principles:

1. Commitment
'Be devoted to one another in brotherly love' (Rom. 12:10). So often 'love' only flows when we satisfy each other's standards, not because it is a basic requirement irrespective of the other's performance. Are you deeply and unconditionally committed to the members of your fellowship on the basis of your oneness in Christ?

2. Love
The ultimate in spiritual experience is love. Note that we are commanded to love. John 13:34 says, 'Love one another.' This implies that true love is not a fitful emotion but a result of deliberate action. Furthermore, Romans 5:5 proves that it is possible to love with the love of Christ — 'God has poured out his love into our hearts by the Holy Spirit'. Love is a basic ingredient of discipleship;

Jesus specified it as the means whereby 'all men will know that you are my disciples' (John 13:35).

3. Transparency

'Walk in the light, as he is in the light' (1 John 1:7), means living transparently with one another and with God so that no wrong spirit, grudge, hardness or negative attitude is allowed to continue and impair relationships. 1 John 2:9, 10 says that we can't be walking in the light if there is a wrong attitude in our hearts to someone else.

4. Humility

The basis of brokenness or meekness is a recognition that we have no rights. Jesus talked about accepting and bearing the cross as a fundamental ingredient of discipleship (Luke 14:27). A cross is a capital 'I' crossed out. Paul talks about being 'crucified with Christ' (Gal. 2:20). Have we ever accepted the cross as a principle? It is the only basis for good personal relationships.

5. Openness

Fellowship also includes a freedom to go to another if we sense a wrong spirit in that person towards us. Of course if we go in a grieved or judgmental attitude we will only makes things worse. Jesus said that if we want to worship the Lord and we know that another person has something against us, then we should seek to re-establish fellowship first. At this point reconciliation has a higher priority than worship (Matthew 5:23, 24).

6. Forgiveness

One of the major road blocks to the flow of the Spirit in one's life is an unforgiving attitude. The need for a forgiving spirit recurs again and again in the Gospels, where it is often linked with effective prayer, for which it is an essential pre-condition. Paul teaches it as an essential ingredient of continuing Christian fellowship. Colossians 3:13 says, 'Forgive whatever grievances you may have against one another.'

7. Forbearance

Jesus recognised that the real crunch in fellowship is maintaining love when another's fallibility is very obvious. Indeed there is not much merit in loving lovable people. Paul teaches forbearance as 'big feeling', or largeness of heart, or magnanimity. In other words, we are to have a 'high tolerance threshold'; this is only possible 'in the Spirit'. Colossians 3:13 again – 'Bear with each other.'

8. Sensitivity

The Lord wants us to be sensitive to the consensus view and to temper strong personal feelings in the light of fellowship attitudes. An overbearing disciple is a contradiction in terms. 'Clothe yourselves with humility towards one another' (1 Pet. 5:5).

9. Communion

Christians are to obey the scriptural exhortation to meet with one another for worship and fellowship. 'Let us not give up meeting together . . . but let us encourage one another' (Heb. 10:25).

10. Encouragement

This is one of the disciple's most strategic ministries. The terms 'exhort' and 'comfort' mean 'encourage'. The references to 'encourage one another' highlight the usefulness of this function (Hebrews 10:25; 1 Thessalonians 5:11; Romans 12:18). The Devil's ministry is the opposite – discouragement and depression.

11. Counsel

'Admonish [counsel] one another' (Col. 3:16). The original word for counsel carries the idea of placing the truth in the mind. A symptom of true fellowship is when a Christian knows he can give a word of counsel or advice (input of truth) to another without fear of reaction. In other words, a bond of trust has been developed which is resilient and does not break, when truth, even unpalatable truth, can be shared in love and accepted in the spirit.

'Competent to instruct [counsel] one another' (Rom. 15:14).

12. Sharing

Actually our English word 'fellowship' is a translation of a Greek word meaning 'mutual sharing of what is held in common' or 'to go shares with'. It is used in Romans 12:13 and 15:27. Discussing what we have learnt about Christ is fellowship; giving of one's substance to another is fellowship; giving time to help others is fellowship; sharing one another's load is fellowship. Galatians 6:2 says, 'Carry each other's burdens.'

13. Restoration

Suppose a serious breakdown in fellowship has occurred. How can it be restored? The Scriptures in Matthew 18:15-22 are very clear. The offended person should go to the other party and seek to have the matter put right. If this can't be achieved he is to go again, this time with two or three others, and if this is unsuccessful he is to lay the matter before the local fellowship of which they are members. We are not to rest satisfied with impaired relationships.

14. Servanthood

Galatians 5:13 teaches that the true expression of the Christian life is a spirit of servanthood – a concern to help one another and a desire to serve one another. Christ washed his disciples' feet, cooked breakfast for them and went about doing good. Paul describes his desire to make himself 'a slave to everyone' (1 Cor. 9:19).

15. Hospitality

1 Peter 4:9 says we are to open our homes to one another 'without grumbling'. This verse shows that our home is a key factor in the cultivating of fellowship. In the qualifications for Christian leadership this attitude is twice mentioned as necessary (1 Timothy 3:2; Titus 1:8) and it is listed in Romans 12 alongside other Christian virtues such as prayerfulness, humility and fervency.

16. Participation

1 Peter 4:10 teaches that one of our fellowship responsibilities is to exercise our spiritual gifts for the benefit of the group. Not to do so is to fail in our function as stewards and to deny the fellowship the blessings which the exercise of these gifts are meant to bring.

17. Unity

Romans 15:5 ('May . . . God . . . give you a spirit of unity') and 1 Corinthians 1:10 ('I appeal to you . . . that all of you agree with one another') teach the responsibility of seeking to find God's mind on an issue. The Holy Spirit does not have two opinions. Voting on a controversial issue (not elections) should be a 'last ditch' measure in a truly Christian fellowship, the ideal being to seek a consensus through prayer and exchange of views, so that clarity and conviction develops in the whole group.

18. Diversity

Unity does not imply uniformity. It is the genius of the Holy Spirit that he equips us all in different ways, and the clear teaching of 1 Corinthians 12 is that while we all have an inescapable relationship to the body, we are each to contribute through our own unique function.

19. Acceptance

Romans 12:10 teaches us to 'honour one another'. Do we only appreciate people when they agree with us? If so, we are guilty of favouritism, which is condemned in James 2:9. A mark of true humbleness of mind is that we 'consider others better than yourselves' (Phil. 2:3, 4).

20. Submission

Ephesians 5:21 makes it clear that we are to 'submit to one another out of reverence for Christ.' The word means to 'place under', and the teaching means that our motivation constantly has to be the other's good, the other's welfare, not our own, out of a fixed acceptance that our priorities are to be Jesus first, others next and ourselves last.

Sweeping? Yes. But totally biblical. 'God opposes the proud but gives grace to the humble' (1 Pet. 5:5).

21. Prayer

A fellowship is only as strong as its members' ministry of prayer for one another. In many local churches especially, this is a great area of weakness; often the prayer meeting has either disappeared completely for lack of support, or degenerated into some less strategic form of gathering. Pray together, stay together! 'Devote yourselves to prayer' (Col. 4:2); 'Pray continually' (1 Thess. 5:17); 'Be . . . faithful in prayer' (Rom. 12:12).

Further reading

The Family of God, Frank Cooke, Henry Walter

Improving Your Serve, Charles Swindoll, Hodder & Stoughton

Love Covers, Paul Billheimer, Christian Literature Crusade

Calvary Road, Roy Hession, Christian Literature Crusade

Friendship Factor, A L McGinnis, Hodder & Stoughton

Knowing Me, Knowing You, Marion Stroud, Pickering & Inglis

Love Has Come Again, Jim Bigelow, Marshalls

20 Reasons Why Disciples Should Be Involved in Cross-Cultural Evangelism

By 'cross-cultural evangelism' we mean the communication of the gospel by members of one ethnic group having its own language and culture to another ethnic group with a different language and culture. For instance, a white Londoner working amongst the Pakistanis would be engaged in cross-culture evangelism even though he is working within the borders of his own country.

1. Christ's explicit command in Matthew 28:19, 20 requires that all nations (Greek, *ethnes* – ethnic groups) are to be reached, discipled and taught.

2. Christ's expectation in Acts 1:8 is that Christian witnesses will go to (a) their own culture (Jerusalem, Judea), (b) nearby similar cultures (Samaria) and (c) dissimilar cultures (the ends of the earth). (See page 100 for further information.)

3. Those who have never heard of Christ are lost. 'No-one comes to the Father except through me' (John 14:6). 'If anyone's name was not found written in the book of life, he was thrown into the lake of fire' (Rev. 20:15).

4. If we value eternal life as our supreme possession, logic demands that sharing the good news about it should

be our supreme concern. 'Go into all the world and preach the good news to all creation' (Mark 16:15).

5. The spiritual principle of generosity as outlined in Proverbs 11:24 indicates we will be better off sharing the gospel than keeping it to ourselves. 'One man gives freely, yet gains even more; another withholds unduly, but comes to poverty.'

6. The teaching of Proverbs 24:11, 12 states that if we have the capability of rescuing the lost and do not do so, we shall be judged accordingly.

7. The world population growth at sixty million a year is far outstripping the growth of the Christian Church.

8. About ninety per cent of the available Christian full-time service force is concentrating on less than ten per cent of the world's population.

9. Only five per cent (about 2,000) of the Church's missionary force is concentrating on evangelising peoples that can only be reached by cross-cultural evangelism (about 2,000 million).

10. The Muslim world of 700 million is, apart from Indonesia, largely untouched by most Christian missions.

11. Only twenty-eight countries in the world are closed to the entry of missionaries for formal mission work. They are: China, Mongolia, North Korea, Vietnam, Burma, Kampuchea, Laos, Syria, South Yemen, Tunisia, Iraq, Libya, Mauritania, Saudi Arabia, Afghanistan, Iran, Russia, Bulgaria, Yugoslavia, Romania, East Germany, Poland, Hungary, Czechoslovakia, Albania, Turkey, Algeria, Brunei, Qatar.

12. Although indigenous churches exist in many countries they form a very small percentage of the total population – usually under five per cent.

13. Many people of the world today are very responsive to the Christian message (e.g. Chinese expatriates, Indonesians, many African nations, and the working classes in many South American countries).

14. Responses from Christian radio, television, gospel magazines, and free gospel newsheets encourage us to

believe that the volume could be much greater if more personnel were available.

15. Urgent requests constantly pour in to mission headquarters from newly emerging national churches, pleading for assistance in training, youth work, and other specialised ministries.

16. Never in the world's history have so many been persecuted for their faith as in the twentieth century. Probably more have laid down their lives for Jesus in this century than in all other centuries combined.

17. The standard of living prevailing in western countries ($4,000-$20,000 per year) gives us a tremendous advantage over our national brethren in underdeveloped countries (average $200-$1,000 per year) in terms of training, mobility and technology.

18. Many countries where missionaries are prohibited or restricted are recruiting westerners with appropriate technical qualifications to aid in their development projects. Qualified Christians should apply!

19. A high percentage of Bible college graduates, having spent three or more years learning theology and communication skills, return to secular life where these abilities are not put to full use. Is this good stewardship?

20. Eighty per cent of the world's population can only be evangelised by Christians who are prepared to cross cultural barriers.

Things to do about this chapter

- Subscribe to a missionary magazine.
- Plan for regular giving to a church-planting agency.
- Enquire regarding the possibility of full-time service.
- Obtain the prayer letter of a missionary/missionary family.

Further reading

Operation World, Patrick Johnstone, STL Books

World Mission in the Eighties, Michael Griffiths, STL
  Books
What on Earth Are You Doing? Michael Griffiths, Inter-
  Varsity Press
Don't Just Stand There, Martin Goldsmith, STL Books
God, That's Not Fair! Dick Dowsett, STL Books

10 *Commandments of Missions*

We often look on mission, at home or overseas, as something of a specialist ministry, only for those who receive a definite 'call' from God. Here are ten commandments from the New Testament that show how involvement in missions is central to biblical discipleship.

1. 'Lift up your eyes' (John 4:3 NASB)
The very strengths of an enthusiastic Christian worker on the home scene – intensity, devotion to his ministry, total involvement – can be weaknesses when it comes to considering overseas missions. It is the hardest thing to detach oneself and begin to take a burden for an area overseas where there is no personal connection. Many times the challenge is in fact swept aside with the comment: 'The Lord's given me the vision and burden for local outreach. Missions are not my scene.' This infers that the lack of mission interest is not his fault.

But the biblical truth plainly stated here by Jesus is that he expects us to lift our gaze from the local and immediate. The action word in the Greek is *epairo*, coming from two roots, *epi*, upon, and *airo*, raise or lift. It is a deep discipline to temporarily push away the local, the immediate, the urgent and seek to have vital concern for a mission, a missionary or a needy people outside of one's own culture. But it is biblical.

2. 'Look at the fields' (John 4:35)

'Take a good look at the fields' says the TEV. And that is a more accurate translation, because the word used for 'look' is not the simple Greek term, *blepo* – it is a word fraught with deeper meaning, *theaomai*. This word is the basis of our word theatre. Now, in a theatre what does the visitor do? Just glance occasionally at the stage or screen? No. A steady gaze, and deep concentration, is what he is engaged in over the next two or three hours. In John 4:35 Jesus is commanding us to take a long hard investigatory look, with a view to interpreting what we see.

'The field' is defined by Jesus in Matthew 13:38 as 'the world'. Attending the church's yearly missionary conference isn't enough. Polite interest in the monthly missionary visitor is totally superficial. The ball is in our court. The Lord expects us to make it our business to find out in detail something of what is happening in the world of missions. In fact he wants us to be world Christians.

What practical steps can be taken?

(a) Visit the local library. Start taking a serious interest in geography and concentrate on one area of the world, at least, for a start.

(b) Write to a missionary society. Ask for their periodical to be sent and offer to pay for it.

(c) If you know any missionaries through personal, church or family links, write to them and ask them to explain what they are doing and why they are doing it.

(d) Buy a copy of *Operation World* (published by Send the Light Publishers) and work through it, noting the spiritual needs of each country. Specialise in one area.

(e) Ask the Lord to lay on your heart for intercessory prayer a missionary, a missionary family, a missionary society, a people, a country, a world area; or a missionary specialist ministry such as radio, literature, medicine, or rural development.

3.   *'Ask the Lord of the harvest . . . to send out workers into his harvest field' (Luke 10:2)*

As in point two, the actual words carry a deeper significance than most of our English translations give. The word, 'ask' is not the simple word to ask or make a request; its truer meaning is 'beseech' or 'earnestly entreat out of a sense of need'.

The words 'send out' are a translation of a verb that has a sense of strenuous, even violent action in it. A truer rendering would be, 'push out, shove, eject'. So a paraphrase of this verse would read, 'Aware of the tremendous need, earnestly beseech the Lord of the harvest to propel workers out into his harvest field.'

Are you obedient to this command? Is it part of your lifestyle? Are you 'sold' on missions? And if you do pray like this do you realise that the proof of your sincerity is your readiness to answer your own prayer?

4.   *'Unless a grain of wheat falls into the earth and dies, it remains . . . alone; but if it dies it bears much fruit' (John 12:24 NASB)*

Here is the law of the harvest – life out of death. And it works in the spiritual harvest also. There is a price to be paid in producing fruit but the result is glorious.

When the young Israelis were entering the service of the priesthood, we learn from Exodus 29 that, having laid hands on a ram, it was slain and some blood brought back and daubed on their right thumb, right ear, and big toe on the right foot. They entered the service of the Lord bearing the marks of death. This was symbolic of the total cessation of an independent lifestyle. From then on they were God's men. If we are to be God's men today we need to listen to his word in 2 Peter 3:9 'He is . . . not wanting anyone to perish, but everyone to come to repentance.' How can we take this verse seriously and not have a heart for missions?

J O Fraser of Lisuland realised that when God called him to inland China, the training in civil engineering which he had just obtained would never be used. He 'died' to civil engineering but he had fruit in hundreds of Lisu families who found the Lord through his faithful service. (*Mountain Rain*, Eileen Crosmann, OMF)

5. *'Christ will suffer and rise from the dead on the third day, and repentance and forgiveness of sins will be preached in his name to all nations' (Luke 24:46, 47)*
It is clear from this verse that it is the will of God that every ethnic group should hear of his love in Christ and have an opportunity to repent and be forgiven. Missions are in the heart of God. He so loved the world that he gave his only son for it (John 3:16). To ignore the yearning of God for the salvation of all lost people is to live a sub-standard Christian life, and to miss the supreme purpose for which God leaves Christians in the world!

6. *'I chose you to go and bear fruit – fruit that will last' (John 15:16)*
Is this 'fruit' simply the 'fruit of the Spirit'? Hardly, because there is no need to go anywhere for that. This passage refers to the impact of our life. Fruit that lasts. This can only refer to the effect of our life and witness on others. The 'go' implies a moving out to reach the lost whether across the street or across the sea.

Jesus positively encouraged his disciples to have a 'harvest' mentality. He said in John 4:38, 'I sent you to reap what you have not worked for.' He said in John 15:2, 'Every branch that does bear fruit he trims clean so that it will be even more fruitful.'

Are you satisfied with ineffectiveness? It's not God's norm. He expects fruit.

7. *'You will be my witnesses in Jerusalem, and in all Judea and Samaria, and to the ends of the earth' (Acts 1:8)*
No part of Judea was more than about fifty miles from Jerusalem. Samaria constituted Judea's northern border, running east-west about twenty-five miles north of Jerusalem and extending for another twenty-five to thirty

miles further north. What distinguished Samaria was that its people had intermarried with surrounding heathen peoples, and because of this, the Judeans rejected their offer of help in the rebuilding of the Temple (Nehemiah). Samaria constituted a different culture and different values but was not vastly different from Judea. The 'ends of the earth' clearly meant peoples who are totally unrelated to us, completely different, with languages and cultures totally new to the outgoing witnesses.

A missions professor called Ralph Winter has termed these three spheres of evangelism as follows:

Jerusalem and Judea	E_1
Samaria	E_2
Ends of the earth	E_3

Every Christian fits into one of these spheres. All of us should be involved in E_1 evangelism. Many will be called to E_2 and some will be called to undertake the more specialised and technical ministry of E_3 evangelism.

8. 'Go into all the world and preach the good news to all creation' (Mark 16:15)

It is important to note the context. In the previous verse Jesus had reproached the disciples for their unbelief. And in the succeeding verse he says, 'Whoever believes and is baptised will be saved.' Clearly they could not bring people to faith if they were still in the wobbly state of unbelief mentioned in verse 14. So the thrust of verse 15 is a call for the obedience of faith. None of us will ever be able to carry out this command in our human strength. The only possibility of compliance is when we see it as an issue of faith-action. The word 'preach' is *kerusso* which really means proclaim. If it were used today it would be the word used to describe the work of a radio announcer.

9. 'Go and make disciples of all nations . . . teaching them to obey everything I have commanded you' (Matt. 28:19, 20)

Only disciples can make disciples. We can't take anyone an

inch further than we have gone ourselves. Jesus plainly saw this as a principle when he said, 'Teaching them to obey everything I have commanded you.' He had put them on the path of discipleship; they were to do the same for others. The quality of their discipling would reflect the quality of their own lives.

The 'nations' mentioned here would not be the political groupings we know today, such as Britain, Germany, United States of America. The word means 'ethnic group' – every group of people with a language and culture of its own.

Notice the sequence of the last three points: witness – proclaim the gospel – make disciples. Each represents a different stage of communication. Our starting point is personal witness but our objective is the discipling of believers so that they in turn become reproducers, capable of creating the full cycle again.

10. *'I urge . . . that supplications, prayers, intercessions and giving of thanks be made for all men' (1 Tim. 2:1 AV)*
Here is Paul's worldwide vision – that Christians 'take on the world' in a four-level prayer ministry. 'Prayers' are just simple requests – 'Bless John Misho as he is learning the Kabala language today, Lord'. 'Supplications' is the translation of a Greek word which has in its root the concept of need. It is more intense than 'prayer' and should be thought of as 'beseech' or 'earnest entreaty' – 'Oh Lord, you know that Mary Misho has had hepatitis and is so depressed. Oh, Lord, reach out and touch her. We earnestly beseech you for her . . .' 'Intercessions' are the deepest level of prayer because the intercessor actually takes on the responsibility for another as a God-given commission, standing between the needy and the Lord and not giving up until the need is met. Moses interceded for the Children of Israel after they had made the golden calf, and told the Lord that he was willing to be blotted out if only they could be given another chance (Exodus 32:32). Jesus is the supreme intercessor, taking on

himself the sin of the world and becoming a mediator for mankind.

'Giving thanks' means we should have a positive spirit, rejoicing in all that the Holy Spirit is achieving in the lives of many men and women across the world, and in the multitudes who come to Christ everyday. While there is still a vast need, we need to balance this with joy and thanksgiving for the mighty workings of the Spirit. More people are coming to Christ now than at any previous age in history.

Further reading

Christian Mission and the Modern World, John Stott, Kingsway

Give Up Your Small Ambitions, Michael Griffiths, Inter-Varsity Press

Student Power in World Missions, D Howard, Inter-Varsity Press

The Chocolate Soldier, C T Studd, WEC

We Believe in Mission, John Wallis (ed.), STL Books

20 *Points on How To Pray for Missionaries*

1. Know the facts

It is difficult to pray effectively unless you understand situations fully. Be prepared to spend time and money in writing to missionaries and obtaining information so that you know the issues being faced, the opportunities being presented and the opposition being encountered.

2. Concentrate

It is impossible to have an in-depth appreciation of a large number of missionary situations. Ask the Lord to show you the one or the few for whom you are to take this responsibility. Establish and maintain a personal link.

3. Know about the mission

Nearly all missionaries are members of missionary societies. Write to their home office and enquire about the principles and methods on which the society operates and the goals they are aiming for.

4. Understand the true nature of the work

Types of missionary service are many and varied. A missionary can be a Bible teacher, evangelist, doctor, administrator, educationist, mechanic, pilot, builder, engineer, etc. But alongside any 'technical' task, the missionary is above all else a soldier fighting in a spiritual conflict against satanic forces. Know the spiritual strategy so you can stand in faith for the advance of the kingdom.

5.   Recognise the factors that oppose

Many factors can lead to the missionary's discouragement. Here are just a few: living in an alien culture, working amongst an unresponsive or hostile people, shortage of personnel leading to overwork, ministry often involving being away from home, tension between the demands of the work and the needs of the family, physical discomfort in sub-standard living conditions, problem-solving and counselling in another language, limited fellowship with others of like mind, government or local official harrassment and for single workers especially, loneliness.

6.   Pray that the missionary will know authority over Satan

Pray that the missionary may learn to resist Satan, taking authority over him, and refusing everything that comes from him. 'The accuser of our brothers' is always ready to suggest that a worker is a failure or is out of the will of the Lord. Christ has given the authority to his servants to enforce this defeat, 'I have given you authority . . . to overcome all the power of the enemy' (Luke 10:19). Satan will not recognise this defeat until forced to do so by the servant of Christ.

7.   Pray for the missionary's spiritual vitality

The key to victory is the missionary's own personal relationship with the Lord. An angry word, an impatient gesture, will mean that testimony is lowered before those he is seeking to be an example to. Ask God to keep workers faithful in personal Bible study and prayer so that the inner man is renewed day by day (2 Corinthians 4:16 NASB). The biggest danger for any Christian servant is spiritual dryness.

8.   Pray for the missionary's physical vitality

One of the biggest snares is overwork. The problem in

missions is lack of personnel. It is so easy to overstretch and to take on too much, so that with insufficient rest, efficiency and health are impaired. Pray that God's servant will recognise the danger signals before it is too late. Pray too for protection from accidents in travel, and from sickness.

9. *Pray for the missionary's mental vitality*
Constantly adjusting to the language and thought forms of another culture can be a wearing experience. Problem-solving in an alien culture brings extra tensions not present when working at home. Pressure of work tempts the missionary to give up reading books that enliven and stretch mental faculties. Absence of a wide (and therefore stimulating) circle of friends can also have a deadening effect. Depression can come through the presence of the forces of darkness. Pray that God's servant may walk in the light of Christ's loving presence and know how to refuse Satan's ministry of depression.

10. *Pray for the missionary's family*
Even when remaining 'on top', many missionary parents have been limited and frustrated by the enemy's counter-attack on his family. Many a missionary father has had the experience of his child becoming sick while he is away on a special assignment. His wife can succumb to loneliness and depression.

11. *Pray for the missionary's attitude to other missionaries*
It may be far harder to love that fellow worker who is always at hand and from whom there is no escape, than the national. God's fullest blessings are realised where there is unity and love between workers.

12. *Pray for the missionary's attitude to the lost*
Again natural love fails to meet the test; often the missionary is not appreciated by nationals who are untouched by the gospel. He is often considered as a foreigner and neither he nor his message are wanted. Only

through patience and love can the missionary win through
to acceptance (2 Corinthians 5:14).

13.   Pray for the missionary's relationship to national Christians

Meekness is the key. In a day of nationalism and increasing
international tension, the only hope for a missionary's
effectiveness is a spirit of humility and a willingness to
work with and often under the leadership of national
brethren.

14.   Pray for a strong national church

The missionary may be forced to leave a country at any
time, but if the national church is established, the work
will go on. The Spirit-filled national is usually more
effective in his witness to his own people than the
missionary. Pray for Bible schools and other means of
training national believers (Matthew 28:19, 20).

15.   Pray for more workers, national and expatriate

We are specifically commanded in Luke 10:2 to pray that
God will 'send out workers into the harvest'. Pray also for
young people in Bible schools at home that they will realise
the need of the fields and respond, and pray for nationals
in Bible schools on the fields. Pray for their teachers, that
they may inspire missionary vision and avoid the pitfall of
merely academic education.

16.   Pray with faith

When God leads you to pray, he means you to pray in line
with his purpose. Prayer is not persuading a reluctant God,
but co-operating with him in his strategy. Prayer should
not be 'asking and hoping' but 'knowing and receiving'.
Mark 11:24 says, 'Believe that you have received it'. Pray
with Christ's delegated authority, i.e. 'in my name' as
instructed in John 14:13, 14; 15:16; 16:23, 24.

17.   Pray consistently and persistently (Luke 11:1-10)

Don't just pray about, pray through, till you reach a place
of confidence, release and praise on a particular issue. Ask

that you be kept consistently sensitive to the Holy Spirit, so that you can enter effectively into the spiritual conflict as and when needed.

18. *Praise God for the answers!*
Don't forget to praise God when answers come, but praise him also 'by faith' before they come. 'Don't worry about anything, instead pray about everything; tell God your needs and don't forget to thank him for his answers' (Phil. 4:6, Living Bible).

19. *Share*
Share your own personal news with the missionary. He'll appreciate knowing about the person who is prepared to identify with him. Likely enough you will go on his prayer list.

20. *Offering practical help*
James teaches us that the reality of our faith is proved by our works. Ask the missionary if there is anything of a practical nature you can do to help. Here are some possible activities:

- Distribution of prayer letters and other relevant information.
- Enthusing others about his ministry and related projects.
- Organising a prayer group.
- Helping to obtain materials for missionary children's education and recreation.
- Sending out up-to-date magazines or books.
- Volunteering to help his mission organisation at home in any way possible.

Further reading

Operation World, Patrick Johnstone, STL Books
The Hour That Changes the World, Dick Eastman, Baker Book House

Rees Howells, Intercessor, Norman Grubb, Lutterworth Press

God's Powerful Weapon, Denis Lane, OMF Books

The Weapon of Prayer, E M Bounds, Baker Book House

Get Your Church Involved in Missions, Michael Griffiths, OMF Books

40 *Factors To Consider About Bible College*

Today, many young people go directly into Christian service for a short-term of one or two years. Organisations such as Operation Mobilisation and Youth With A Mission encourage this and offer short discipleship courses at the start of the period.

However, many of these returning from such work have caught the vision of full-time long-term service and are more open to consider some form of Bible training, because the inadequacy of their Bible knowledge and their limitations in counselling and cross-cultural communication have been highlighted during short-term service. Nevertheless, deep reservations about the practical value of Bible college training are held by many.

Tremendous variations

Before attempting to list advantages and disadvantages it must be stated that Bible colleges vary tremendously, both in curriculum content, academic standards, and practical relevance; also college staff vary too in terms of interest in and promotion of service at home or overseas. The tone of Bible colleges vary from country to country. Canadian schools have a strong missions emphasis. Some colleges in Australia don't. Many colleges in Europe espouse an academic approach, those in Britain tend to be fairly balanced both in mission interest and practical emphasis.

The type of college the writer considers as satisfactory is one offering a good spread of Bible and Bible-related subjects, over a two or three year course. It will be manned by a staff of wide experience, deeply committed both to missions and to the needs of the home churches. The course will offer not only studies but guided practical experience in conjunction with local churches and agencies.

Bible college? No!

The following arguments *against* Bible college training have been heard from time to time:

1. The experience of many young people who go to college is that they lose the intensity and desire that they previously had for the things of the Lord.

2. Being shut away from the normal pressures of secular life produces an artificial spiritual 'hot-house' environment which can lull participants into a false sense of spiritual development.

3. Many find that the nature of the studies undertaken are unrelated to daily living and have no practical implications for them.

4. A very close level of fellowship results in awareness of each other's shortcomings and this often leads to time being wasted on inter-personal squabbles.

5. The artificial distinction between 'staff' and 'student' leads to a 'two-tier' pattern which tends to produce a 'cover-up' attitude in both parties.

6. The evangelistic outreach is usually compulsory so that natural spontaneity and enthusiasm is killed.

7. The inevitable 'patterning' of ideas and concepts which is prevalent in any school where there are staff members with strong convictions, leads to students being

influenced towards adopting these patterns without genuine personal conviction on their part.

8. Success is usually tied to examination results rather than to the issues of life that are less tangible and less easy to assess, such as spiritual maturity and equipment for ministry.

9. Conformity to a rigid structured programme does not in itself bring maturity. Many react afterwards and return to an undisciplined lifestyle.

10. The graduate's future is largely (and often unfairly) determined by the final assessment compiled by a college staff member and given to the organisation to which the graduate applies.

11. Most college staff members tend to be specialists in a narrow field of knowledge rather than people who have proved themselves in the hurly-burly of Christian experience over a reasonable period of time. Hence the approach to service tends to be academic rather than practical.

Bible college? Yes!

On the other hand, here are some definite advantages of Bible college training:

12. To get the maximum out of training means making the most of the time available. A structured programme is good for the person who is not naturally well-organised or disciplined.

13. The close-knit fellowship of a Bible college campus provides a valuable level for long-term fellowship and interaction between people of different backgrounds, so that maturity in inter-personal relationships is developed.

14. The strong emphasis of a good college will be on a practical grasp of spiritual principles – principles that will affect values and lifestyle. Unhurried grappling with such issues like personal discipline, intercession, creative faith, authority, etc., lead to a greater readiness to cope with life situations.

15.   An in-depth knowledge and understanding of the Scriptures will lay a groundwork for on-going satisfactory Bible study, and for the training of others in meaningful Bible study.

16.   Participation in college life will inevitably require submission to authority at various levels. This is an invaluable discipline.

17.   Bible college experience also usually means participation in Christian service under controlled conditions. The student's effectiveness can be evaluated and help given leading to improvement.

18.   The total Bible college experience will also enable the student to discern where his/her spiritual gifts lie. This provides a valuable indication of the type of service in which to become involved afterwards.

19.   Most colleges encourage visits from leaders and workers of various Christian missions and organisations. The vision for service is therefore widened, and a greater knowledge of world conditions gained.

20.   Interaction with sympathetic staff becomes the basis of accurate and productive counsel for the student, based on the staff's intimate knowledge of the student's life and performance. This is a tremendously potent force in the student's personal development.

21.   Most schools are now including missiology in their curricula; this gives valuable insights into effective methods of evangelism and church growth.

22.   The challenge of local involvement in outreach and other church-related activities heightens the awareness of the spiritual conflict involved in Christian service and this can lead to valuable experiences in prayer and intercession.

23.   Only in a situation like a resident Bible college can folk get away from the 'tyranny of the urgent' and give themselves time to consider the 'importance of the strategic'. The very fact that a regular time with God every day is possible and encouraged, helps students to grapple with issues they might never otherwise face.

24.   Most interdenominational missions and

organisations have a firm policy of requiring that applicants complete a minimum of two years residential full-time training at a recognised Bible college. The Bible college certificate is a passport to service with most missions. (A few missions offer their own in-service training programmes.)

25. It has come to be recognised in recent years that communication is a complex skill, and cross-cultural communication even more so. It seems wise therefore to have the specialised training which most colleges offer, so that the new worker will be able to communicate effectively. This fact is relevant to numerous Christian activities such as preaching, teaching, counselling and writing. Other associated subjects like homiletics, pedagogy and ethics give students exposure to the problems of relating Bible knowledge to specific areas of life and ministry. (The reaction of most Bible college students after their first year is, 'I never knew how much I didn't know . . .')

What next?

If you are thinking seriously of Bible college training here is a suggested sequence of actions to take:

26. Ask your pastor or local Christian bookstore manager for a list of the colleges in your country.

27. Write to three or four asking for a prospectus, and from it carefully evaluate:

- the programme
- the policies
- the financial position
- the practical experience given to students.

28. Try to discover (or write to the college and ask for the address of) a recent graduate and find out how a student assesses the college.

29. If you intend working with a particular mission or organisation, ask whether you would be acceptable to it

after graduating from the college you have in mind. Or ask them which college they recommend.

Questions to ask

Try to get answers to the following questions about the school you have in mind:

30. Are its staff members in demand for ministry in the churches?

31. Is the school having to make constant appeals for money?

32. Does the graduate list for the last five years reveal whether the highest percentage is moving on into Christian service or returning to secular life?

33. Do societies readily accept graduates or require them to have more training elsewhere?

34. Do churches seek out graduates for help as youth pastors, deaconesses, etc.?

35. Are overseas students welcomed and given help?

36. Does the college offer a follow-up counselling service to graduates?

37. Are staff members experienced in Christian service as well as holding academic qualifications?

38. Do the staff and students relate well, e.g. sharing in meal times, prayer times, recreational activities; or are the staff isolated from student life?

39. Are staff members readily available for personal counselling?

40. Are staff members committed to missions? Have any of them worked with a missionary organisation?

This whole issue deserves very careful thought, consistent prayer and self-less decision making.

Counsel from others can be really helpful if it comes from mature people with a vision for world evangelism, but beware of those who are out to promote their own local group or who play down missionary zeal because of their own lack of concern.

Further reading

Many missionary biographies show the relevance of prior training. Some give illustrations of how to be a good missionary without it!

In the first category are Brother Andrew (*God's Smuggler*), Don Richardson (*Peace Child*), Isobel Kuhn (*One Vision Only*), Fenton Hall (*Hero & Pioneer*).

In the second category are the lives of Bruce Olson (*For This Cross I'll Kill You*), J O Fraser (*Mountain Rain*), Paul White (*Alias Jungle Doctor*), C T Studd, Norman Grubb (*Once Caught, No Escape*).

11 *Principles About Church Health and Growth*

The Scriptures warn disciples against living their lives in isolation. Hebrews 10:25 says, 'Let us not give up meeting together'. So discipleship means identification with a local Bible-believing church fellowship and participation in its activities. Concern for the health, well-being and growth of this fellowship should rate a high priority in the disciple's life. Here are some well-established principles of church health and church growth.

1. Commitment to each other

The basis of a healthy (and therefore growing) church fellowship is the individual members' commitment to one another on the basis of Christ's express command to 'love one another' in John 13:35, and not on the basis of individuals' predetermined standards of acceptance. ('Her dress is too short'; 'His hair is too long.') This area of commitment means that we accept as paramount the necessity of absolutely genuine honesty and transparency in our relationships with each other, and we 'keep our accounts short' in terms of putting right anything that comes in to darken our 'walk in the light' (1 John 1:7).

2. Leadership awareness and concern for growth

When the leaders of a church come to accept the fact that lack of growth is a curable disease, then they will be willing to face up to any hindrances to growth that are present, such as prayerlessness, lack of concern for the lost, worldliness, disunity or apathy. Concern for growth should produce an honest appraisal of the church's effectiveness in outreach.

3. Positive thinking

The church's leaders must become convinced about the possibility of church growth. If they do not rise in faith and expectancy regarding growth, the church will not grow. Commitment to the concept of growth will often lead the leadership to exercise faith for growth and to take practical steps with this objective in view. (See points 9 and 10 for a description of these.)

4. Free and joyful worship

Surveys have shown that outsiders are attracted to worship services when these have a warm praiseful atmosphere. This is very different from many traditional services in which the atmosphere is impersonal, formal and heavy. A praise section using Scripture choruses and well-known hymns, a prayer section in which requests come from the participants and a testimony section in which individuals are free to praise God for something, are features that are often present in growing churches.

5. Body life

Fellowship is minimal in a formal service in which all the activity is by one person in one place. If a church of more than fifty retains a formal worship service some other provision has to be made for the personal interaction of members on a regular basis as an integral part of the church life. This will often require the setting up of informal Bible study groups, and the training of leaders' for them. These often turn out to be the 'growing edge' of the church as newcomers are attracted to the informal sharing times.

6.   *Membership participation*

Growing churches need the involvement of rank-and-file members in the running of their activities. Every Christian has at least one spiritual gift so there is something for every member to do that will benefit the body as a whole. Wise church leadership maximises the potential of its members, and helps individuals discover and use their spiritual gifts.

7.   *Vital intercession*

Lasting growth is dependent on the existence of a group of people who know how to pray. There is a difference between praying 'about' and praying 'through' or prevailing prayer, such as Jesus taught in the story of the insistent householder who badgered his neighbour for bread in Luke 11:5-8. This type of prayer seldom takes place within the confines of an average 'mid-week service'. Some with a knowledge (or willingness to acquire a knowledge) of spiritual warfare will need to make time to evaluate the present scene, discern God's strategy, and to pray through to victory. The church leadership also needs to make time for this kind of praying as distinct from 'business'. This usually requires an early morning meeting once a week.

8.   *Missionary concern*

When a local church genuinely accepts the Great Commission as an integral part of church life, and starts to plan boldly for the giving of money and the giving of their own personnel for world outreach, God starts to pour out his blessing. Growing churches keep the mission field constantly before the people, and have times of special emphasis such as an annual missionary convention or a monthly missionary service.

9.   *Local outreach*

There is no 'prize formula' but concern for growth usually leads to an examination of the ways in which outsiders can be reached. This can be through evangelistic Bible studies in homes, youth outreach, guest services, pinpointing community needs (old people, the unemployed, or migrant groups), and seeking God's way to reach them. One church appointed a staff worker to work specifically with unemployed youth. Result – growth. Another realised it had three old people's homes in the vicinity so they organised services for them and arranged transport. Result – growth. Still another opened a child-minding centre in the hall which was adjacent to a shopping centre. Result – growth.

10. Growth starts with an honest evaluation of the church's past and current performance

Study the membership roll over the past twenty years. Plot a graph of years against membership numbers. Find the percentage growth rate over a period of time. (If a group of one hundred adds twenty members in five years this is a twenty per cent growth rate for the five year period, or an average annual rate of four per cent.) Study any peaks or valleys on the graph and ask 'why'? Ignorance of past performance is not a virtue. Prayerfully consider what a reasonable 'faith-growth' project would be for the next three years.

Alongside a willingness to probe and evaluate there must be a willingness to change.

11. Growth principles taught

Although primary responsibility for change lies with the leaders, a new programme cannot simply be 'landed' on the congregation. A time of education on church growth principles is essential before initiating change. And change is most effective when the decision is made by all those who are going to be involved, not just the policy-makers. Otherwise the congregation can be polarised. What if a few do maintain an entrenched position, defending the status quo? A choice has to be made between stagnancy and 'moving with the movers'.

Further reading

I Believe in Church Growth, Eddie Gibbs, Hodder &
   Stoughton
Church Alive!, Peter Cotterell, Inter-Varsity Press
Can My Church Grow? Martin Goldsmith, Hodder &
   Stoughton
All Change, Michael Saward, Hodder & Stoughton
Step Into the Sunshine, Derick Bingham, Pickering &
   Inglis

9 *Ministries For Mature Disciples*

Here are nine avenues of Christian service in which experienced, mature, stable disciples can make a most significant contribution:

1. An 'investment' ministry (New Testament model – Barnabas)
Your greatest resource is your maturity. Therefore your prayer should be, 'How can I invest my spiritual knowledge and understanding in younger Christians? How can I disciple them?' The pattern for this is given in 2 Timothy 2:2 where Paul says, 'The things you have heard me say . . . entrust to reliable men who will also be qualified to teach others.' This will mean considering the following steps:

(a) Praying about whom you can encourage.
(b) Learning to identify meaningfully with them, and having them in your home.
(c) Quietly taking them 'under your wing' for fellowship, counselling and encouragement.
(d) Praying for them.

Note the 'encouragement' ministry of Barnabas in Acts. He encouraged Paul when other Christians rejected him

(9:26, 27). He encouraged the new converts in Antioch (11:22-24). He took Mark with him on a second missionary journey when Paul would not (15:38, 39).

2.   A prayer ministry (New Testament model – Epaphras)
Four levels of prayer are mentioned in 1 Timothy 2:1 where Paul says, 'I urge . . . that requests, prayers, intercession and thanksgiving be made for everyone'. The deepest level is intercession. The intercessor accepts responsibility for the spiritual welfare of another. Epaphras 'agonized' in prayer that the members of the Colossian church may be mature and completely confident about the will of God (Col. 4:12).

Possible targets of intercessory ministry could be:
(a)   People with obvious spiritual needs in your church or fellowship.
(b)   Christian leaders – pastors, elders, deacons, youth leaders.
(c)   Missionaries.

You can also be a catalyst in stimulating prayer for mission groups and evangelistic agencies.

3.   A home ministry (New Testament model – Aquila and Priscilla)
The New Testament describes how homes were used for evangelistic meetings, spiritual instruction, hospitality for Christian workers, prayer meetings, personal counselling and church services.

Have you realised how strategic your home could be for the kingdom of God? for a neighbourhood Bible study? a place for Christian youth to meet on a Saturday night? a venue for a children's mid-week meeting? a centre for a branch church?

See how Aquila and Priscilla used their united testimony and home facilities to extend God's work. We read of churches meeting in their home (Romans 16:3, 4; 1 Corinthians 16:19). They gave hospitality to Christian workers (Acts 18:2, 26).

4. A supporting ministry (New Testament model – The Philippian Church)

If you are in the thirty-to-sixty age bracket you are in the group which is normally the most capable of providing adequate support for God's work and workers. Have you examined the scriptural teaching on tithing in the Old Testament? And giving in the New Testament? 2 Corinthians 9:6-14 shows that giving should not be in unpremeditated spurts, but planned carefully. Note what the Scriptures promise to the generous person in Proverbs 11:25, 'A generous man will prosper; he who refreshes others will himself be refreshed.' You can't beat God at giving.

Ask God to show you where your contribution can be most productive for the extension of God's kingdom. Give special attention to those who are directly involved in evangelism and church planting. Paul wrote to the Philippian church, 'I am amply supplied now that I have received . . . the gifts you sent. They are a fragrant offering, an acceptable sacrifice, pleasing to God' (4:18).

5. A community ministry (Old Testament model – Joseph)

Christians are desperately needed in the social and political life of the nation. Your life, testimony and influence could affect community standards for the better. Christian voices are needed at all levels of government. Membership of a parent-teacher association can mean affecting school programmes and standards. The need of the socially disadvantaged is a wide field for Christian endeavour.

Joseph's testimony and ability profoundly affected the Egyptian nation. Read the enthralling story (in Genesis 41) of how he became prime minister and saved the nation from the effects of a seven year famine.

6. A leadership ministry (New Testament model – Titus)

Your local church needs leadership. If you are spiritually mature be open to consider the service of leading. You can serve your local fellowship by accepting a leadership role.

(See chapter 24 for a development of this function.)

Titus had the administrative ability and discernment which led Paul to ask him to stay in Crete. He was to sort out some problems and appoint elders (Titus 1:4, 5). Paul also writes about him in 2 Corinthians 8:17, 'He is coming to you with much enthusiasm and on his own initiative.'

7. A cross-cultural ministry (New Testament model – Luke)

Do not let age rule you out of a possible cross-cultural ministry. Many Christians in their thirties, forties and fifties are going overseas today in the capacity of:

(a) Short-term workers (usually those who can fill a specialist or technical 'slot' without needing to learn a language).

(b) House parents and teachers in missionary children's schools.

(c) Host and hostess or manager/manageress in mission headquarters or fellowship centres.

(d) Accountants, printers, and builders who can work in a mission support capacity. (Many other trades are useful, too.)

It is also possible to have a cross-cultural ministry within your own country by reaching out to immigrant groups and overseas students.

Luke was a doctor who joined Paul's mission band and travelled widely in church work. He also did the Christian church a great service through writing a Gospel and the book of Acts.

8. A representative ministry (New Testament model – Tychicus)

Outside of major cities, most missions and interdenominational agencies depend heavily on local representatives. Here are some of the activities which can help stimulate interest and concern:

(a) Organising prayer cells.

(b) Arranging meetings and transport for visiting speakers.

(c) Maintaining a display for use in churches and youth groups.

(d) Promoting sales of literature provided by the organisation.

(e) Generally enthusing others for a missionary/evangelistic cause.

(f) Providing or arranging hospitality for visiting representatives of the mission group.

Tychicus was Paul's representative on numerous occasions – in Ephesus, Colosse, and perhaps Crete (Eph. 6:21; Col. 4:7; Titus 3:12).

9. A counselling ministry (New Testament model – Paul)
The word often translated 'warn' or 'admonish' in our Bibles is from a Greek word which strictly translated means 'to place in the mind'. Paul says in Colossians 1:28, 'We proclaim him, admonishing [counselling] and teaching everyone . . .' He also says to the Colossian Christians, 'Let the word of Christ dwell in you richly as you teach and admonish [counsel] one another . . .', (3:16). He says to the Corinthians, 'I am not writing this to shame you, but to warn [counsel] you' (1 Cor. 4:14).

Paul describes his ministry to the Ephesian church in these terms, 'For three years I never stopped warning [counselling] each of you night and day . . .' (Acts 20:31).

Further reading

The ABC of Follow-Up, Ron Smith, STL Books
From Now On, Ralph Shallis, STL Books
Take My Silver, Peter Maiden, Paternoster Press
Life Style Evangelism, Joseph Aldrich, Marshalls
Christian Leadership, John Perry, Hodder & Stoughton
A Friend in Need, Selwyn Hughes, Kingsway
Strategy for Living, Dayton & Engstrom, Gospel Light

4 *Fundamentals of Spiritual Leadership*

Most Christians who follow the path of true discipleship eventually find themselves on the ladder of leadership, whether it be on the lower rungs with a Sunday school class, home Bible study group or youth club; or on the higher rungs of eldership or even pastoral responsibility.

This chapter seeks to clarify the four basic responsibilities of leadership as revealed in the New Testament.

The starting point is Acts 20:28 where Paul says to the leaders of the Ephesian church:

NIV	Colloquial English	Key Word
1. Keep watch over yourselves	Guard your own testimony	DEED
2. [Keep watch over] all the flock	Care for the people	HEED
3. of which the Holy Spirit has made you overseers	You are Spirit-appointed guides	LEAD
4. Be shepherds of the church of God	Make sure the people get spiritual nourishment	FEED

Summarising the four responsibilities in descriptive terms, we could say that leadership means functioning:

as *models* (giving a good example through the quality of our lives)

as *guards* (exercising a caring and protective ministry)

as *managers* (directing the affairs of the fellowship)

as *shepherds* (ensuring that the people obtain spiritual teaching).

A study of the seven leadership passages of the New Testament* reveals that the key words in each passage fall very naturally into one of these four categories.

Although leaders may have gifts that make them more effective along one line of activity than another, the Scriptures place all four responsibilities squarely on each person. There can be no opting out of caring even though our gift is organising.

What activities belong to each of the four basics? Here are some suggestions:

1. Example

If our witness is weak or inconsistent we can forget about the rest. Remember, that people evaluate our formal message (what we say) by the para-message (what we are). The para-message is made up of our attitude, credibility, approachability and sincerity. We always communicate in stereo — by saying as well as being.

2. Caring

No care without prayer. A leader who doesn't carry a prayer list of his group is a non-leader. The key to effective intercession is identification, or empathy. We can only pray with feeling and accuracy when we understand people intimately. That takes time for visiting and knowing in depth.

This section also includes practical matters such as giving hospitality and practical help in the ordinary affairs of life. One pastor found that chopping wood for some old people stimulated more spiritual concern than many of his sermons.

3. Managing

The leader should be an initiator, a person of vision, able to discern God's purposes and to communicate them to team members for their consideration. He must know how

*Acts 20:17-35; 1 Thessalonians 2:7-13; 1 Timothy 3:2-5; 4:12-16, 5:17; Titus 1:1-8, 2:1-15; Hebrews 13:7,17; 1 Peter 4:1-3.

to plan, how to use and develop the resources of his team, how to motivate people and how to organise and channel energies towards the achievement of agreed goals.

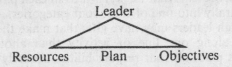

Leader

Resources   Plan   Objectives

If he is a leader in a Christian organisation such as a church or mission, his team will probably consist of volunteers for whom financial reward is not a motivating factor. He needs to be a 'people' person, sensitive to the reactions of others. Jesus said, 'I am among you as one that serves' (Luke 22:27). The good leader recognises that he serves his team by leading it.

4. Feeding

The shepherd does not necessarily provide the food but he must know where his people can get it and encourage them to utilise it. A gift of teaching is not implied in the Scriptures – only readiness to share known vital spiritual principles in an informal way. Counsel, advice, correction and discipling are all implied in this term, so the responsibility is clear – the leader needs to have a solid grasp of truth himself, 'so that he can encourage others by sound doctrine and refute those who oppose it' (Titus 1:9).

Further reading

Spiritual Leadership, J Oswald Sanders, Marshalls
Christian Leadership, Derek Prime, Pickering & Inglis
Competent To Lead, Kenneth Gangel, Moody
Managing Your Time, Engstrom & Mackenzie, Zondervan
The Making of a Christian Leader, Engstrom, Zondervan